Supervision and Leadership in Childcare

GU00985586

Supervision and Leadership in Childcare

Eileen Mc Partland

Gill Education
Hume Avenue
Park West
Dublin 12
www.gilleducation.ie

Gill Education is an imprint of M.H. Gill & Co.

978 07171 5342 8

Index compiled by Cover to Cover
Print origination by O'K Graphic Design, Dublin
Printed and bound by CPI Group (UK) Ltd, Croydon, CR0 4YY

The paper used in this book comes from the wood pulp of managed forests. For every tree felled, at least one tree is planted, thereby renewing natural resources.

A CIP catalogue record is available for this book from the British Library

Dedication

For Seamus

Acknowledgements

Books happen because of great people in the background, who support, cajole and silently work miracles!

In appreciation of my place in the process, I would like to offer my sincere thanks and appreciation to: my family for the grounding; Michael King, Ann O'Donohue, Una Mc Entaggart and Linda Mc Loughlin, for support; work colleagues and students at Liberties College for patience and enthusiasm; Kareen because of what she stands for; Marion, Catherine, Anita, Kristin, Jane and all the team at Gill & Macmillan, who are the most understated miracle workers I know.

Contents

ONE

Early Childhood Care and Education (ECCE)

There have been significant developments in the lives of children in Ireland in recent years, and the emergence of the Early Childhood Care and Education (ECCE) scheme is one such advancement. The development of a new approach ensures that the care and education of young children is now combined and supported by government. Every pre-school child from birth to age six in the country, regardless of background, ethnicity, culture or ability, will receive a quality learning and nurturing experience which will stand to them for life.

Following considerable research and consultation on the early childhood of our youngest citizens, *Síolta, the National Quality Framework for Early Childhood Education* and *Aistear: The Early Childhood Curriculum Framework* were developed to guide practitioners in the emergence of a comprehensive strategy towards the provision of a development and learning framework for our children by setting out principles, goals and structures that support the work undertaken with pre-school children. These must therefore become a significant part of the work of any supervisory position in the care and education of our children. With them comes the responsibility to ensure that all the standards outlined are met and supported by all and that in doing so the interests and rights of all children are met. These must become working documents in any childcare or education setting and will inform the position and work of any leader or supervisor in the sector.

Síolta

Síolta, the National Quality Framework for Early Childhood Education is a set of principles and standards relating to the quality of the care and support of young pre-school children in whatever setting they are found. It sets out 12 **principles,** which are interdependent and comprise:

1. **Valuing** early childhood in every child's life.
2. Putting **children** first.
3. Including **parents** in interactions and dealings in relation to children (interestingly, it refers to parents and makes no distinction between parents, carers and guardians).
4. Building meaningful and positive **relationships** that support the child.
5. Treating **equality** as a fundamental part of meeting every child's needs.
6. Ensuring that **diversity** is valued and recognised.
7. Ensuring that the child enjoys an enriching, quality and stimulating **environment**.
8. Overseeing a safe and secure setting that protects the child's **welfare**.
9. Ensuring that the **adults** involved in a child's early childhood are suitably qualified and motivated to create a quality experience for each child.
10. Sharing and co-ordinating proper **team** structures for all involved in the child's care, education and support to achieve the best results for each child.
11. **Pedagogy** marries education and care so that neither is pursued at the cost of the other.
12. Making **play** central to each child's rights in all early childhood settings.

(A useful mnemonic for remembering these 12 principles is **TRAPPED PEW** is Very Comfortable).

These goals help define quality in early childcare and are incorporated along with 16 **standards** of quality to be attained in settings, each of which can be assessed and together allow others to judge the quality of a setting. They form a type of quality assurance process for early childhood care, with the child at the centre of any such analysis.

The 16 Síolta standards, which are collated as components, are envisaged as setting a standard of delivery for a well-rounded approach to early childcare and education. Each component has subcomponents that can relate to the different levels of each component and in some cases relate to the different stages of development of the children in the setting, such as the component relating to the rights of the child (Standard 1). In this component, the subcomponents ensure that the provider meets the rights of the child, in the case of a baby by observing the child's preferences, and later, when the child is capable of articulating their preferences, by listening to the child. This is fitting in relation to the concept of each child reaching their best potential at each stage of their development.

Fully implementing and supporting the 16 standards in any setting would indeed mean that every child would receive holistic early childhood care that is supportive and enabling. However, it is also clearly stated in Síolta that these standards are the responsibility of every person who is involved with the child in whatever capacity, and as such, they must become a fundamental part of every supervisor's everyday life in a childcare and education setting.

The 16 standards of Síolta are as follows.

1. Ensuring that the **rights** of the child are foremost in the child's care and education.
2. Ensuring that the **environment** (including materials and equipment) is of a high enough standard to support, protect, stimulate and challenge each child.
3. Ensuring that families and **parents** are part of the child's support systems and that there are policies and procedures to confirm that this is the case.
4. **Consultation** with all stakeholders, including children themselves and their families, should support inclusive, informed participation and decision-making.
5. All **interactions** in children's lives, whether with other children or with other adults, should be supported by policies and be child centred and child enabling.
6. **Play**, whether with other children, adults or alone, should be safe and appropriate to the child's needs from a social or developmental point of view.
7. **Curriculum** should be flexible, holistic and based on the needs of the individual child and the principles of child development.
8. **Evaluation** and planning should be ongoing, informed and reviewed to inform practice in the setting and the life of the child.
9. The **health** and welfare of each child should ensure that they are protected, nourished, secure and respected in the setting.
10. The **organisation** of the setting should be clearly informed by written philosophy-inspired policies, procedures and guidelines.
11. **Professional practice** should ensure that everybody who works with children has sufficient knowledge, skills and appropriate values and supports to provide an enriching experience for the child.
12. **Communications** with, and in respect of, children should be clearly supported by appropriate policies and procedures to protect the interests of the child.
13. **Transitions** should be clearly managed and supported for children, whether in or between settings.
14. **Identity**, belonging and empowerment should be encouraged to enable each child to develop a sense of self.
15. **Legislation** and regulations should clearly inform practice.
16. The **community** around the child should be open and accessible to the child and the setting and interactions should be facilitated and supported.

(Another mnemonic to assist you in remembering these significant standards is **PHILPOTs RECIPE** Cooks Cup Cakes.)

Aistear

Aistear (Irish for 'journey') is a curriculum framework for those involved in the early education of children. It sets out the way in which all those involved in childcare will work together to create a holistic approach to the early education of pre-school children in whatever setting they find themselves. Aistear explains its purpose as 'providing information for adults to help them plan for and provide enjoyable and challenging learning experiences so that all children can grow and develop as competent and confident learners within loving relationships with others' (National Council for Curriculum and Assessment, 2009). Not surprisingly, Aistear also sets out standards of support that children can now expect in their early learning experiences.

Aistear is based on 12 principles, which are set out in three groups. This assists the understanding of and approaches to learning using this new curriculum framework.

Group A: Children and their lives in early childhood:
- The child's uniqueness
- Equality and diversity
- Children as citizens

Group B: Children's connections with others:
- Relationships
- Parents, family and community
- The adult's role

Group C: How children learn and develop:
- Holistic learning and development
- Active learning
- Play and hands-on experiences
- Relevant and meaningful experiences
- Communication and language
- The learning environment

When compared with either the principles or standards of Síolta, it is easy to see that Aistear supports the achievement of Síolta's goals in the daily lives of children in a setting and supports the professional child practitioner in their daily work. Aistear recognises that children may receive their care and education in a variety of settings and provides examples of how its principles can be achieved in a number of such settings. It is clearly a curriculum-based approach to the achievement of its stated principles and as such should be seen as a sample of what can be incorporated rather than the limit of what is needed. In the foreword, Batt O'Keefe TD, the Minister for Education and Science, described it as a curriculum framework that 'can contribute greatly to helping our youngest citizens grow up with a strong sense of well-being; proud of themselves, their families and communities; confident and competent communicators; curious and resilient explorers; and creative thinkers' (National Council for Curriculum and Assessment, 2009).

Both Síolta and Aistear will become the guides for every practitioner in the early childcare and education setting, and a supervisor in such a setting has a responsibility to understand all that is involved in the delivery of a holistic child experience as outlined in these ground-breaking publications. The easiest way to describe the connection between Síolta and Aistear is that Síolta draws a picture of what early childcare and education should achieve and Aistear gives working examples of how practitioners might go about putting some of the goals into place in the day-to-day work that is carried out with children in the setting. Neither Aistear nor Síolta stands alone and neither should be seen as the ultimate answer. Just as every child develops individually and differently, so should the concept of the care of that child. Every practitioner should be open to new ideas to challenge and enable children and every supervisor should be reflective and open enough to consider the infinite possibilities of using curriculum to enhance children's learning, and to support staff in exploring such possibilities towards a truly quality childcare and early education system in Ireland.

Embedding Síolta and Aistear

As you can see from Figure 1.1, this new approach to childcare is multi-layered and all the principles, standards and themes are interlinked. This is the first comprehensive description of how the profession of childcare will move to one of childcare and early education. Therefore, it is not surprising that those who work within the sector will require significant skill sets at this important time in children's lives.

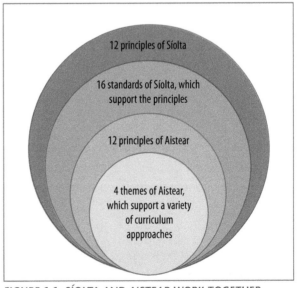

FIGURE 1.1: SÍOLTA AND AISTEAR WORK TOGETHER

The skills involved in the delivery of care and support as a supervisor in an ECCE setting are numerous and wide ranging and include the following (see Figure 1.2).

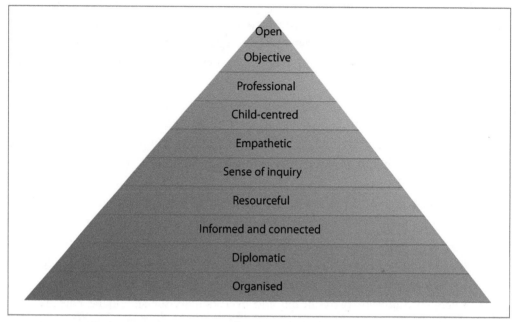

FIGURE 1.2: THE BUILDING BLOCKS OF THE SUPERVISOR'S ROLE

Openness

The supervisor is required to be open to current and proposed developments in the ECCE sector so that changes to standards can be quickly and efficiently interpreted and implemented. While things may be working well in a setting, small changes or the addition of a new child or staff member can change some of the dynamics and the supervisor must be open to the possibilities and/or challenges this may bring.

Continual challenge and thought should produce a supervisor who is willing to support staff, children and parents so that every child reaches their potential. Additionally, they should be open to suggestions as to how to bring new concepts to their own setting, which enables staff to develop to their best potential and creates a dynamic, fun, well-functioning workplace where everybody feels they belong.

Objectivity

The supervisor will be required to look at the holistic (whole child) nature of an ECCE setting and how positives may present themselves, and indeed how everything can be a possibility or opportunity. Decisions need to be made in the best interests of the child, which requires the supervisor to approach things with an objective frame of mind.

At all times, the supervisor should look at everything involved in the setting and how decisions impact on everybody, including how problems, if left unresolved, can create a dysfunctional workplace where resources are used unproductively. Everybody has a place in the setting and an objective supervisor often facilitates the way in which everything comes together and creates a smoothly working, welcoming and happy learning and caring setting.

Professionalism

By their very nature, childcare and education are professions, and there are norms of behaviour in such professions that must be maintained and which affect the approach the professional takes to tasks and situations. Being reflective is a fundamental component of that professionalism, and to realise how one's actions can impact on others is an important part of being reflective, which will be discussed later in this book.

Professionalism also brings with it norms of behaviour and ethics which will be firmly established in any setting. Maintaining privacy, supporting children with specific needs and leading a well-structured, highly motivated team is a challenge in any childcare setting, and the professionalism of the leader or supervisor should make everybody feel supported, enthused, valued and well informed on the day-to-day running of the setting.

Child centred

This is imperative, as in ECCE the child needs to be consulted and supported while growing to a position where they will be capable of becoming aware of their own abilities and support structures. In Síolta and Aistear, this is a strongly valued skill, as the child needs to be placed firmly at the centre of all activities in a truly holistic approach. In the new approach to ECCE work, the needs, preferences and views of children are not just considered but are actively sought, developed and encouraged; which also fits into the goals of the United Nations Convention on the Rights of the Child (UNCRC).

Children are individuals with different cultural backgrounds, ethnicity, abilities, needs, preferences and family orientations. This indicates the depth of information to be taken into account when aiming to be child centred in your approach, but at its very heart it means putting the child first in all aspects of running the childcare facility and ensuring that children's best outcomes are always considered.

Empathetic

In order to understand the impact of decisions on children and their families in an ECCE setting, the supervisor should be familiar, open and responsive to the feelings of the people involved in the dynamics of the setting. All stakeholders are required to be considered, which means that the supervisor must allow themselves the time and space to understand what the impact of their decisions might be on those affected.

Compromise may be needed in some situations so that everybody is happy with choices made, and a good supervisor or leader will be able to negotiate compromise where it suits best. There is therefore a need to be able to understand the feelings a decision may evoke in a person, and this is where empathy is most relevant as a skill in the work of the supervisor.

Sense of enquiry

The supervisor needs to be motivated to enquire about developments in the sector, but must also be open to opportunities to change things themselves for the betterment of children and all stakeholders in their own particular setting. Possibilities should be just that – not seen as a challenge, but rather as a chance to see if things can be achieved within boundaries.

No supervisor is ever always going to know exactly what to do in new situations that arise in their workplace, and the ability to investigate and enquire about possible solutions is a necessary skill. This enquiring mind must also be able to see if the situation as it appears is correct and that things are not being misinterpreted where problems arise.

Resourcefulness

It is inevitable that challenges will present themselves in an ECCE setting, and with a number of stakeholders. These challenges may need to be faced on a daily basis, whether from a child's education or care point of view or an administrative point of view. The supervisor is challenged to provide answers and this in itself requires the supervisor to be aware of a range of solutions that can be explored.

This resourcefulness may extend to getting funding for things that need to be done in the setting or indeed creating opportunities for children in the setting to go on outings, visits or adventures, which can create valuable learning opportunities for all the children and staff. Getting things done requires skills of resourcefulness, especially when things go wrong and problems need to be negotiated.

Informed and connected

The supervisor will need to be able to work in multidisciplinary teams where the work of various professionals may need to be balanced and supported in the interests of the children in the setting, either individually or collectively. Networking and being able to make connections at different levels will support this work and requires the supervisor to set up their own networks and information banks. Access to information and membership of professional organisations will form a big part of this challenge.

Connectedness also refers to being connected to the implications of your own decisions for others and being attuned to responses that may lead you to review decisions you have already made. In some situations, it is simply a matter of looking at the situation from another angle, deciding that the new circumstances require a different outcome, knowing you are in a position to make the necessary change and deciding to do whatever is required.

Diplomatic

Whenever the needs of varying groups have to be balanced in favour of one over the others, there is a need for diplomacy. This can be viewed as the ability to put across a point of view that might conflict with an already held view or indeed might require the existing view to be radically changed. Compromise and negotiation are fundamental parts of the skill of diplomacy and this is necessary in ECCE settings.

The ability to tell a parent that they are doing/not doing something that will impact on their child, while retaining the respect and trust of that parent, requires a diplomatic approach. This skill may take time to acquire. Knowing when to speak and indeed how to put things in a way that will not cause offence can often defuse a difficult situation and, more important, may bring about results that are in the best interests of the child in your care.

Organisation

Leading, forming, supervising or changing teams and their dynamics requires organisation. Observations, information, skills, staff qualifications, policies, procedures, legislation, regulation, finances and resources must be properly recorded and balanced, which means the supervisor must be capable of putting in place proper reporting and recording procedures that contribute to the smooth running of the ECCE setting.

We will discuss more of these supervisor skills and tools in the following chapters, but the one thing that will support all these skills is stamina. It is not a job for the faint-hearted.

TWO

Reflective Practice

Reflective practice is a fundamental part of the work of a childcare professional. Using the term 'professional' presumes a set of standards, competences and achievement goals for you as a member of an industry. One of the most important of these is putting the child at the centre of everything you do and ensuring that their welfare is your top priority in your procedures, practices and behaviours.

This is not just an ideal, as you will see in Chapter 16 on legislation, as you are legally obliged to put the best interests of each child you work with at the centre of all you do in childcare. This means that whenever you look after children in your care, you must be aware of how everything you do impacts on the child and how important it is for you to be responsive to the needs of the child. You are also responsible for ensuring that you understand what it is a child needs to reach their full potential, which will certainly affect how you behave, act and react in your professional life.

An illustration of how complex is this process of putting the child at the centre of everything can be seen in Figure 2.1, which is not exhaustive but shows what is involved in looking at the child as an individual, a learner and a fundamental part of the service you provide.

Never underestimate your role and contribution to the life and well-being of a child, but just as important, never underestimate the complexity of your job and the learning process you undertake in childcare.

Reflection is like a weaving process that takes account of all these interacting factors between the children you care for and the job you do. Being what is called a reflective practitioner is about understanding:

- Your caring responsibilities.
- The worth of your own abilities.
- The limit of your abilities in any given situation.
- The importance of your role in the life of a child.
- Your contribution to the team you work with.

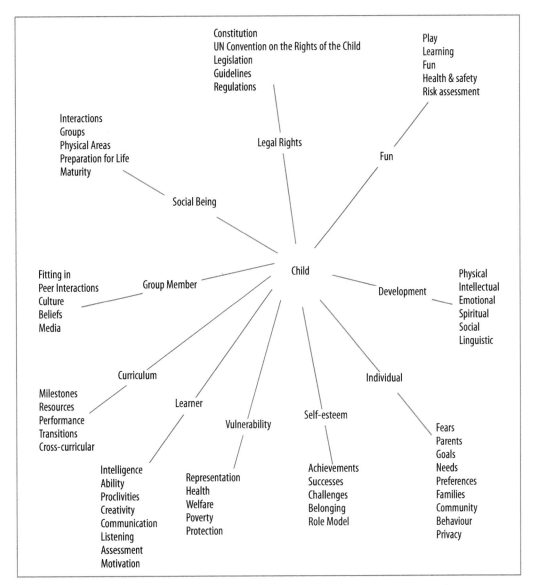

FIGURE 2.1: THE COMPLEXITY OF THE CHILD

- Knowing that challenges change on a daily basis.
- Accepting that you are accountable for your own actions.
- Acknowledging that you are continuously learning.
- Accepting that professionalism means committing to quality performance standards and competences.
- Being open minded and keeping abreast of new methods, advancements and technology in your profession.
- Accepting that childcare is not just a job, but is a constantly evolving concept.

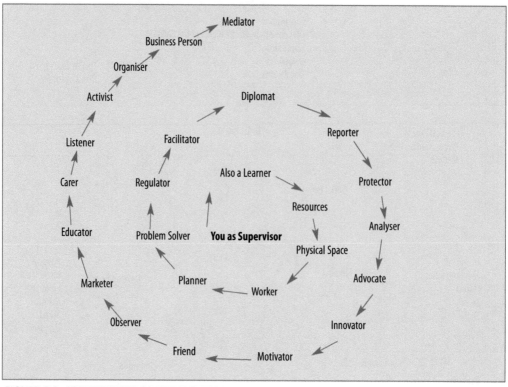

FIGURE 2.2: COMPLEXITIES OF THE SUPERVISOR'S ROLE

While it is necessary to embrace all these complex concepts, it is fundamentally just as important that you are aware of your own strengths and weaknesses in the process of reflection. Knowing your limits and challenges is highly important in an industry where you care for vulnerable individuals.

Reflective Portfolio Activity

1.   List five strengths you feel you have.
2.   List five weaknesses you feel you have.
3.   Ask a friend to complete step 1 and step 2 about you.
4.   Ask a family member to complete step 1 and step 2 about you.
5.   Compare the three sets of strengths and weaknesses you now have.

You will be surprised at the differences you find in the lists – in particular, you will more than likely find that you have underestimated your own strengths. The difference in the lists is about how we view ourselves more critically than others do. This exercise allows you to be a little more objective.

You now have a realistic and informed picture of your abilities and limitations, but remember, this is based on your own honesty in the process!

There is nothing wrong with having weaknesses – we all have them. The reason they are examined in this way is to acknowledge where you might need to put procedures in place to bypass your own weaknesses. For example, if you are not good at dealing with conflict you may need to get some experience through reading or doing a course that would add to your skills in this aspect of your work. Another thing you may have put on your weakness list could be that you procrastinate (most of us do), so you may need to put a list system in place (you can also use your mobile phone or computer) so that things get done on time. The benefit of actually putting a solution in place to overcome something you are not very good at (to the extent that you would describe it as a weakness) shows a proactive approach, which is expected in managers and supervisors.

Another reason you would look at your skills in the above way is that sometimes you are viewed by others as being better at a skill than you think. If you look at this more closely, it may be a skill that would be useful in more situations than you have thought about. This kind of approach is behind the concept of being a reflective practitioner. Over time, you will learn to put things in logical, realistic sequences, which can inform your next actions.

While working in childcare means working in a caring profession, the process of reflection is about *you* – how *you* did things, what *you* needed to improve on, how *you* might do things differently next time and what outcomes would be affected if *you* changed *your* approach. This can be relevant when you come across a new challenge with a particular child and may not come across the same problem until years later. If you have noted down what you did at the time, you then have something to refer back to for clues on how to deal with the problem or how to go about finding a solution – this is like building your own reference manual.

As part of your Level 6 childcare qualification you are required to keep a journal of your learning experiences and this is the basis of a reflective journal, which every childcare worker and supervisor should keep over their career. It is not just something you do until you get your qualification, but should become a working document for you for all your years in the profession. The notes you take one day may become relevant 10 years down the line.

A fundamental ingredient of meaningful reflection is setting aside the time and space in which to carry it out. You can undertake reflection:

- As you walk home from work.
- As part of a winding-down process.
- In the quiet of the evening.
- On the bus/train as you travel to and from work.
- As part of a structured process in your workplace.

- Using a prompt list, as given in the next example, as a starting point until the process becomes seamless.
- Using a diary or just a notebook, which becomes a working 'live' document.
- On your computer as a continuous narrative about your work.

Over time, a reflection process undertaken in this way will become a therapeutic process that can help you unwind after challenging days or can even be a means of acknowledging what you achieved on any particular day. While children may be a significant part of each day's reflection, there may be times when staff, parents, processes, resources or even procedures become the focus of your thoughts. The concept applies to everything you do in your professional capacity, and by doing this you are becoming an active player in your own learning.

Students often find it difficult to start a journal, as they feel self-conscious about what they write because it will be read by others as part of the learning experience. After qualification, however, for the most part your working journal will only be read by you. This means that over time, you will become more fluent in how you approach what you write. However, until this confidence develops, the following prompts will help you to establish a habit that will serve you well and allow you take an objective view of what you encounter in your work.

This list is not exhaustive and some questions may be more relevant than others for the type of facility you work in. Some of the things you might want to reflect on may not arise in other scenarios, but over time and with practice, you will develop your own style of reflective focus, which will become your consistent style. It is useful to date your journal/diary, as this gives you a contemporaneous record that can be referred back to in a particular timescale (this is especially important in cases of referral to other professionals, as might arise in child protection issues), where your notes may well form the basis of an evidence trail in the future and are effectively dated by the order they have in your journal – other things are written later, which proves that the notes you refer to were taken on the date being quoted.

Reflective Portfolio Activity

Possible prompts for your reflective journal:
- What happened in your work today? (Give a summary of the key points.)
- How did what you have already learned help with your day?
- Did you notice any relationship between things that happened and what theorists say about the things you encountered?
- How did what you already know benefit the children you worked with today?

> ▸ Did you learn anything today that could be of use with another child/children you work with?
> ▸ How would you go about trying this out?
> ▸ How did your own personal strengths and weaknesses show in what you did today?
> ▸ What did you learn today that would make you a more effective childcare worker or supervisor?
> ▸ What challenged or worried you in your work?
> ▸ What might you undertake to make your performance better?
> ▸ Is there somebody you can/should consult about what happened?
> ▸ Is there anybody who could help? How would you go about getting that help?

If you start to write as if you were answering these questions in your journal, you will see that in order to answer them, you must be very tuned into what you did – this is what it means to be a good reflective practitioner. The process feels strange and you might feel self-conscious when you first start, but over time it becomes part of what you do and therefore becomes more natural and meaningful for each individual childcare worker.

Used effectively, the reflective journal can be part of your goal-setting strategies for up-skilling and professional development by highlighting what *you* recognise as your learning goals based on actual needs you identify in the process involved. This could help you focus, therefore, on specific skills and courses that are needed immediately and thus give quick returns in terms of the time and effort you put into your own professional development. Over time, you may observe other professionals you work with successfully solving a problem that has been bothering you, and making a note of their methods can be a form of peer learning for you. Alternatively, you can solicit the assistance of a more experienced practitioner in another setting who may be of help in suggesting solutions to problems you encounter.

As a practitioner in childcare, you will be required to consult with other professionals as part of your ongoing work with the children in your care. These experiences become part of a network you might use again in the future, especially if a problem being dealt with happens again. This interaction can give you a new focus on how a problem or challenge might be dealt with in relation to a child. It may well also point to training needed for your staff, which will be of benefit to everybody in your setting. You might need to budget for training to support the professional development of staff under your supervision in order to bring efficiencies to your workplace.

It is also important to remember that your style and the effectiveness of your reflection will differ throughout your career. You might think slowly and methodically when you start out in childcare, but after a while you will become more confident in your own abilities and observations and your style of reflection will change accordingly.

Reflective Portfolio Discussion Activity

Jennifer is caring for a four-year-old child who is displaying very challenging behaviour that is affecting other children and is very upsetting to watch.

Discuss how Jennifer might feel about dealing with this situation and what her concerns might be in her reflective journal. Think about how she might write about the situation and how she might go about getting advice in each of the following scenarios:

(a)   As a student on work placement
(b)   As a newly appointed supervisor
(c)   As a supervisor with 10 years of experience

As a leader, you should encourage all your staff and trainees to engage in reflective practice and establish times and interaction opportunities that will allow for enriching learning in your setting. If you encourage such a commitment to reflective practice in your service, you will be setting the stage for an informed and committed staff who have much to offer children in your setting for years to come and who feel supported and confident in their practice.

Throughout this book there are portfolio activities for you to undertake and reflect on so that you can become familiar with a range of tasks you will be using in a supervisory position in an ECCE setting. These tasks are designed to make it easy for you to complete the activity, while the process of reflection is up to you, as all reflection will be in your future working life. They should form learning opportunities that you will be able to build on in your setting and to look back on later in your career when you need new direction or understanding.

THREE

Children's Rights

Síolta's Standard 1 reminds us that 'ensuring that each child's rights are met requires that she/he is enabled to exercise choice and use initiative as an active participant and partner in her/his own development and learning'. There are many concepts in this standard that every ECCE setting must adhere to so that the child is reaching their best potential. However, while the child will not actually be taught the law, it is important that they understand that they have choices and can make them in a safe and supportive environment.

UN Convention on the Rights of the Child (UNCRC)

This important agreement between world states has been ratified by Ireland, and by doing so we undertook to incorporate its core elements into our laws, thus becoming part of a worldwide approach to children's rights. There are four core elements to the Convention:

- That children will not be discriminated against in any laws we write.
- That the best interests of the child will be taken into account in every law relating to children.
- That every child has the right to life, development and survival.
- That we will respect the views of children.

By ratifying the UNCRC, we undertook that all of our laws in relation to children must incorporate these four concepts from the date of our ratification.

The Convention regards a child as somebody below the age of 18 unless otherwise stated in the laws of the state. We have now adopted this definition across our laws.

Throughout its Articles, the UNCRC sets out the commitments of every state ratifying the Convention to have due regard to the traditions, cultures, values and background of every child, the opinions of children in so far as they do not harm others and are taken in the context of the age and stage of development of the child, and the idea that children should be protected because of their vulnerable position in society.

The provisions touch on every aspect of a child's life and as a supervisor you must take into account these rights in the way you approach your work. There is a children's version of the UNCRC and this could be displayed in the setting. You and your staff should be familiar with the content of the Convention, as every law we pass will be based on its ideals.

Irish Constitution

The Irish Constitution sets out the basis of all rights in Ireland that are imprescriptible (cannot be taken away even if we don't use them). Our Constitution is divided into Articles, which set out the basis of each right. These can only be changed by a referendum of the people who by majority vote may change the provisions of each Article.

In the Constitution at Articles 41 and 42 we find details in relation to children in Ireland. Article 41 states that children are protected in the family and that the mother is given a special position because of the work she does in the family. Article 41 has important significance in childcare as it guarantees that the child's family must be consulted on things that relate to the child. In childcare, this Article is the basis of our concept of *in loco parentis* (you are in the place of the parent), whereby parents must have a say in the care of their children.

Article 42 states that the parents are the primary educators of their children and have the right to make choices in relation to that education according to their means and beliefs. Additionally, it says that the state must provide every child with a primary education. This Article allows parents to choose what provision they will make for their child's education and ensures that choices made regarding that education in whatever context will be the parents' choice.

Both of these Articles affect the way we approach parents in the setting and prompt us to include parents in our activities in relation to childcare and early education. Síolta specifically reminds us in Standard 1 that we must take into account the preferences of the child but also that both the child and the adult are equal partners in the care of the child in the setting.

Acting *In Loco Parentis*

We have seen from the above that there is a duty of care when working with children to do so as if we were taking the place of the parent in the setting, but that the parent must be consulted on everything to do with the child. This significantly influences the way things are done in any pre-school setting.

The parent must have a say in the way things are done in the setting and the duty of care is as if it were the parent giving that care. This means more than simply justifying things that we do by saying that a parent would do the same. It means that the duty of care must be agreed upon by the parents and that there is consultation on an ongoing basis with those parents.

In Síolta, under Standard 4 on Consultation, there is a requirement to seek contributions on decision-making from a wide range of stakeholders and to act on those contributions. However, it should never be the case that the stakeholders (which include staff and others) have a say greater than that given to parents under our Constitution or that the concept of in loco parentis can be ignored just because other stakeholders are consulted.

Child Care Act 1991

This Act sets out the framework for the care of the child in our society and in the process also gives responsibility to what is now known as the Health Services Executive (HSE) to represent the state in relation to the care and welfare of all children.

The Act also set out our system of protection of children and how instances of abuse are reported and children dealt with in the process. We now know that many arms of Irish society did not comply with this Act, which led to the publication of *Children First: National Guidelines for the Protection and Welfare of Children*, which was updated in 2011.

The Child Care Act 1991 states our commitment to the care and welfare of all children and to the constitutional rights of every child in Ireland to be cared for in the family. The Act tries to balance these rights with the UNCRC by stating that the child's best interests will be protected and only in cases of immediate danger will the Gardaí take a child from their family, and even then the process must go before a judge to be agreed upon.

The Child Care Act also provided for the Childcare Regulations, which set out the standards to be maintained in the setting, as we will see in later chapters of this book.

Child Care (Pre-School) (No. 2) (Amendment) Regulations 2006

Regulations are a way of setting minimum standards. They can be changed more quickly than an Act of government, which must go to each house of the Oireachtas for approval and can take considerable time in the process.

The Regulations, as we will see in subsequent chapters of this book, require that standards of care throughout childcare in Ireland are suitable for the care of vulnerable children. They set out what records must be kept (under Regulation 5) and set minimum standards in relation to health and safety measures; ensuring safety procedures are in place; qualification of workers; and space for children provided in an ECCE setting.

As a supervisor you must have a copy of the Regulations on the premises at all times, along with the Child Care Act 1991 and other pieces of legislation as they are enacted. Every setting must keep records of children's activities, as we will see later in this book, and it is the supervisor's duty to oversee this.

National Children's Strategy

The National Children's Strategy was written to put the care and welfare of all children on the island of Ireland in context. It sets out standards of involvement for children and encourages children to be facilitated to play an active part in their own society.

Children must be consulted and allowed to have a say in accordance with their age and stage of development, as set out in the UNCRC above. One of the first developments after this strategy was published was to include children on committees (e.g. Dáil naÓg) to help them understand how their rights are protected. This allows children to learn how they can change things for their own good and also that they have a responsibility to contribute to the development of society.

One of the first developments after the publication of the National Children's Strategy was that children asked that the playgrounds in parks be reinstated following a period of being dismantled for insurance reasons. The Strategy is a model of how consultation can be incorporated into children's everyday lives, as will be done in every pre-school setting by staff and supervisors.

Letting Children Have a Say

It is important that children are listened to in any setting, particularly since the ratification of the UNCRC, which is, as already stated, incorporated into the standards of Síolta and Aistear.

Children should be given opportunities to voice their opinions and this can be done by talking to them directly, by allowing them to vote on things that happen in their setting and by including them at a level that is appropriate to their age and stage of development. Children play an active part in their own development but are due an extra duty of care that you as supervisor are charged with providing.

When considering activities for children in the setting, you should allow interaction and introduce the concept of choice so that a child learns to have their own say, which can be developed over time. In doing this, the child should also be encouraged to consider how their choices might impact on others. By incorporating these standards into the daily activities of the children in your care, you are providing the foundations of good citizenship for the future.

FOUR

Creating the ECCE Environment

G ood preparation work in a childcare and education setting creates an environment where things run smoothly and children and staff are happy and reaching their best potential. However, this is not achieved simply by opening the door. Before an ECCE setting is operational, quite a lot of planning and preparation are required and there are organisations that must be consulted and officially put on notice of your intentions in the process. First, however, an operator of a childcare facility must be absolutely sure of what is involved in running a good childcare facility and must make a realistic assessment of their motivations, skills and abilities in setting up such a business. This is not a business for you if you are not prepared to embrace it with a dedication that will see you through.

Choosing the Facility You Want to Operate

The decision to start a childcare business is usually the start of a journey through a multifaceted industry, as there are different forms of service you may choose to operate, as described by the Child Care (Pre-School Services) (No. 2) (Amendment) Regulations 2006.

Childminding service

This is described as 'A pre-school service which may include an overnight service offered by a person who single-handedly takes care of pre-school children, including the childminder's own children, in the childminder's home for a total of more than 2 hours per day, except when the exemptions in Section 58 of the Child Care Act 1991 apply.'

Factors that may influence your choice of this service include:

- It is based in your own home.
- There is a space requirement for each child so that they can stretch, crawl and play.
- No more than five pre-school children (including the operator's own pre-school children) can be minded at any one time.
- There is a limit of two children under 15 months (with exceptions being made for multiple births or siblings).
- The childminder must have a phone.
- There must be a second person available to deal with emergencies.
- The service is very much dependent on the childminder themselves – if they get sick, it may cause severe difficulties.
- Your own children are included in the maximum number of children that may be looked after under the Child Care Act 1991 and the Child Care (Pre-School Services) (Amendment) Regulations 2006.
- The small number of children allowed may limit the resources of the childminder.
- The small number of children may mean that each child gets more individual attention.

Sessional pre-school service

This is a service offering a planned programme to pre-school children for a total of no more than 3.5 hours per session. Services covered by this definition include pre-schools, playgroups, crèches, Montessori pre-schools, naíonraí, notifiable childminders and similar services that cater for pre-school children.

Factors that may influence your choice of this service include:

- A shorter time in the setting may suit younger children.
- Children are not overburdened.
- It allows for variety in a child's day so that they can do other things during this time which are not in the pre-school service.
- This may be suited to parents who work part time and do not require a full-day service.
- It may facilitate parents who cannot afford a full-time service.
- An operator may be able to offer two sessions during the day and thus cater for more children in a day.
- The floor area per child requirement is $2m^2$ per child aged 0–6 years under the 2006 regulations.
- The adult/child ratio is higher than with a childminder but lower than a full day care setting.

TABLE 4.1

Age range	Adult to child ratio
0–1 year	1 : 3
1–2 ½ years	1 : 5
2 ½–6 years	1 : 10

- The maximum number of children who can be in one room in a sessional service is 20, subject to space and area required for each child under the childcare regulations.
- This type of service may suit people who only want to work part time themselves and may prefer to have only one session per day.
- The requirements to have facilities, etc. can prove expensive for an operator who is limited to the number of children who can use the service.

Part-time day care service

This is a pre-school service offering a structured day care service for pre-school children for a total of between 3.5 hours and 5 hours per day and which may include a sessional pre-school service for pre-school children not attending the full day care service. The service must provide the same physical environment, including rest, play and sanitary facilities, as for full day care. Services covered by the above definition may include pre-schools, playgroups, crèches, Montessori pre-schools, naíonraí, notifiable childminders and similar services that cater for pre-school children.

Factors that may influence your choice of this service include:

- Children are not overburdened during their day and can still have time in the day that is not spent in a service.
- The child still benefits from structured planning in the activities undertaken in the service.
- The service must provide the same facilities as if it were a full-time service.
- Economies of scale are harder to win, as the income to expenditure on the facilities is slower to break even.
- The space requirement per child under the 2006 regulations is as follows:

TABLE 4.2

Age of child	Floor area
0–1 year	3.50 m²
1–2 years	2.80 m²
2–3 years	2.35 m²
3–6 years	2.30 m²

- The adult/child ratio for this service is the same as that for a full-time childcare service.

TABLE 4.3

Age range	Adult to child ratio
0–1 year	1 : 3
1–2 years	1 : 5
2–3 years	1 : 6
3–6 years	1 : 8

Full day care service

This is a pre-school service offering a structured day care service for pre-school children for more than 5 hours per day and which may include a sessional pre-school service for pre-school children not attending the full day care service. Services such as those currently described as day nurseries and crèches are included in this definition. Where a full day care service also caters for children who do not attend on a full-day basis, the adult/child ratio and group size for sessional services should apply.

Factors that may influence your choice of this service include:

- If you are building a service facility, it means you can offer a full range of services throughout the child's pre-school years, such as baby, wobbler and toddler services.
- This service may include an after-school service, allowing children to stay with the service for many years and providing support after they have started school.
- A child's siblings may be in the full day care service and can interact with the child during the day.
- There may be an expectation of discounts from parents with more than one child in the service.
- Meals are usually part of the expected service. This can bring its own pressures in relation to staffing, food safety and other regulations.
- There is usually a strong community connection because of the number of children and the length of time they spend in the service during their young lives.
- The adult/child ratio is the same as for the part-time day care service (see Table 4.3).
- The space requirement per child under the 2006 regulations is as follows:

TABLE 4.4

Age of child	Floor area
0–1 year	3.50 m²
1–2 years	2.80 m²
2–3 years	2.35 m²
3–6 years	2.30 m²

Pre-school service in a drop-in centre

This is a pre-school service offering day care, which is used exclusively on an intermittent basis. It is a service where a pre-school child is cared for over a period of no more than 2 hours while the parent or guardian is availing of a service or attending an event. Such services are mainly located in shopping centres, leisure centres or other establishments as part of a customer/client service.

Factors that may influence your choice of this service include:

- The location is usually leased from the builder of the centre where it is located and the operator does not usually incur building costs.
- It may be open all day but may not be busy all day. Numbers may be hard to predict, so some children may be turned away at certain times if the service is full.
- It would not usually offer food, as the children are staying a maximum of 2 hours.
- The space requirement per child under the 2006 regulations is $2m^2$ per child aged 0–6 years of age.
- The adult/child ratios are as follows:

TABLE 4.5

Age range	Adult to child ratio	Group size
Full age integration 0–6 years	1 : 4 1–4 children where no more than two are under 15 months per 1 adult	Max. group size 24

- These services are relatively new in Ireland and parents may prefer to take the child with them to do the shopping, etc.
- There is a presumption that this is a highly subsidised service, so parents may not want to pay above a certain level, as it is secondary to their main activity in the location.
- Can be isolated for the operator in quiet times.
- Hard to predict staffing requirements at some busy times in the year.
- Times of opening may be determined by the facility it is connected to, e.g. late night opening hours in supermarkets.

Pre-school Service in a Temporary Drop-in Centre

This is a pre-school service offering day care exclusively on a temporary basis. It is a service where a pre-school child is cared for while the parent or guardian is attending a once-off event such as a conference or sports event.

Factors that may influence your choice of this service include:

- The difference between this and the drop-in centre above is that the child can stay for the duration of the event the parent is attending.

- You must give at least 14 days' notice before running such a service at an event such as a conference.
- There is usually no continuity of service after the event has finished.
- It is usually offered on a cost-neutral basis, as the event is the main attraction.

Overnight pre-school service

This is a service in which pre-school children are taken care of for a total of more than 2 hours between the hours of 7 p.m. and 6 a.m. except where the exemptions provided in Section 58 of the Child Care Act 1991 apply.

Factors that may influence your choice of this service include:

- It is not very common in Ireland and thus may take a long time to establish a clientele.
- The ratios are as follows:

TABLE 4.6

Age range	Adult to child ratio
0–1 year	1 : 3
1–6 years	1 : 5

- At least one member of staff must be awake and actively supervising and checking on the children at all times. Where this is not practical, electronic baby monitoring and occasional actual checks may suffice.
- A maximum of five children can be catered for, which includes the childminder's own pre-school children.
- There must be a telephone on the premises and a second person to cope with emergencies.

This is not a comprehensive list of pre-school services. It excludes community crèches, au pairs and other arrangements, which would, however, normally fit the general descriptions above and have similar limitations and considerations.

In all of the above examples, the adult/child ratios are the maximum and may actually be amended downwards by the HSE depending on the clear space available for each child in the service to have space to spread about. Where such a reduction does take place, the operator will be notified and given a reason. The operator may make representations, but where the decision is upheld it applies for the future running of the service unless something changes.

Notification

Once you have decided what type of service you wish to offer, you should go about planning the facility you envisage, making sure that all planning limitations and requirements of your local authority are adhered to. A good architect will ensure that you meet the specifications of the Building Control Act 1990 and 2007 and Building Regulations 1997–2006. Your architect would ideally have a pre-planning meeting with your local authority so that any limitations or specific aspects you are planning can be discussed and teased out. Obviously, planning permission must be sought, as required by law. Potential problems can be spotted in such pre-planning meetings before plans are submitted, which can prevent costly errors or redrawing and means that materials, drainage systems, ventilation, emissions, access for disabled persons, soundproofing, stairways, etc. meet the building regulations and do not pose problems for planning.

Considerations that should be taken into account at this stage include:

- Internal and external finishes.
- Parking and set-down for parents.
- Buggy storage for parents who wish to leave buggies for collection later.
- Inside and outside play areas.
- Landscaping, gates and fences.
- Width of doors and corridors.
- Interaction space inside the premises.
- Accessibility.
- Adaptability of space and usage issues for disabled children and adults.
- Drainage and sewerage systems.
- Waste disposal and storage areas.
- Recycling areas.
- Lighting, ventilation and heating systems.

Síolta provides a good checklist for any person to prompt an architect in drawing up plans. Standard 2 on setting the environment helps you to consider many things under each age category of child in the pre-school environment and can be a good checklist as you design your premises in relation to age, ability, size, hazards, housekeeping items (laundry, etc.), floor coverings, surfaces and textures throughout.

Síolta also encourages you to consider the multiplicity of use of areas within the pre-school service for providing stimulation, challenges, interactions, performance, quiet areas, display areas, wet areas and all-weather accessibility of areas.

Initial consultation with the HSE at this stage can save additional heartache if some element of the design has to be changed to satisfy the HSE inspection and regulation requirements for the proposed service, as they will be the deciding body in relation to suitability for purpose.

Additionally, the Fire Officer for your area should be informed of your intention to open a pre-school service and will undertake a preliminary visit to check that there is adequate access for emergency vehicles in the event of an incident at the service. Under the Fire Services Act 1981 and Fire Safety in Pre-schools Guidelines 1999, the Fire Officer will check that fire alarms and smoke detectors, fire blankets, extinguishers and other safety devices are adequate for your requirements and suitably placed and that your internal announcement systems are adequate to deal with any issues that may arise. You should have a proper emergency plan in place to evacuate the building in the event of a fire, which can be reviewed by the Fire Officer, as well as sufficient procedures in place to prevent a fire in the first place. Failure to satisfy the requirements of the Fire Officer could stop your service opening despite your best plans and considerable expenditure.

It is also advisable to have your architect consult with the Food Safety Authority (FSA) at this stage to check that any physical requirements they may specify are included in your kitchen plans, as changes later on can add to your expenses before you start to make money in your service. Being informed is cost effective from the beginning and changing layout plans on paper is much less expensive than modifying a building that has been completed.

In this process you should also look at the versatility of what you are proposing for your service. Children, parents or staff may have particular needs that are best considered at the beginning so that costly adaptations are not necessary later. The fire alarm you fit may need to have a flashing light attached to warn deaf people of danger, and you may be able to adopt a Braille signage system so that people with a visual impairment can find their way around. Things like this are best considered at the time of development, as they can be easily incorporated into a tender document and costed by a quantity surveyor along with door specifications, toilet sizes, etc.

Where you are not involved in the building of a service and are leasing or part of a franchise, the level of detail is no different – it is about your vision and making that a reality. In the case of a franchise operation, much of the vision is given to you in the franchise documents, as there is a uniformity of appearance and standards in such operations. However, if you are buying an existing establishment, you should carry out your own due diligence to ensure that the requirements of the regulations have been satisfied. Also check if there are any restrictions in the planning already in existence. This may prove beneficial, as the planning can sometimes allow longer hours than are being used and may even include Saturdays and Sundays, which can offer possibilities for future development.

Having secured planning permission or bought/leased an existing or newly built facility and satisfied the requirements of the Fire Officer, you are then required to officially notify the HSE of your intention to open a pre-school facility. To do this you must fill out the required form at least 28 days prior to your intended date of commencement (the exception being the temporary drop-in service mentioned above, where 14 days' notice is required). The details of the form to be filled out giving notice to the HSE is included in the Child Care (Pre-School Services) (No. 2) (Amendment) Regulations 2006. After such notification, the HSE will arrange for an inspection to be carried out to ensure that the service satisfies all the requirements under the regulations.

This is a very detailed inspection and as a student you should look at the Pre-School Inspection Tool on the HSE website (www.hse.ie) to see what is examined and the detail involved. This is a useful resource in the planning process for any pre-school service and is also an excellent tool as part of ongoing quality assurance processes in your service. The ideals are set out and each service is measured against these. It is not required that every single criterion be met in the inspection, but the weighting and consideration given to non-compliance issues will determine whether your service poses a risk to children in your care and is therefore not suitable for purpose. During this inspection, the HSE will also determine if your adult/child ratio will differ from those set out in the regulations as outlined above. Every inspection is followed by a report to let the designated person in charge get feedback on the inspection, and suggestions are detailed as to how compliance can be achieved where there is a need highlighted by the inspection. It is proposed that a copy of the report will be published on the HSE website in the future, which would become part of the information available for parents who are choosing a service for their children.

There is an annual fee payable to the HSE to fund such inspections, which must be paid by the operator of the premises. Inspections take place regularly to ensure continued compliance. It is advisable to work with the HSE on any remedial actions needed after such an inspection, as failure to do so can lead to your premises being declared unsuitable – and a listing on a website as a premises that does not comply can have serious implications for your service. A willingness to comply will be recorded and some of the issues noted are often easy to rectify with consultation.

As a new setting, you must also notify the FSA if you propose to serve food in the setting. The FSA will carry out inspections to check that you are complying with food safety legislation in relation to serving facilities and food preparation and storage requirements. Details of notification are available at the FSA's website (www.fsai.ie).

In relation to safety in your premises, you also need to check out www.hsa.ie on the need to have a safety statement and to see if any hazards can be avoided at planning stage. All these websites make it easy in a planning phase to avoid many foreseeable problems that can be costly to rectify later.

Equipment

An essential part of the image and functionality of your service will be centred on the equipment and resources you choose for it. Every piece of equipment you put in your service will have multiple effects on and uses by the children and staff in your setting. Each piece will add to the overall experience for every child, so it is important that you are aware of the contribution your choice of equipment has in your setting and its value to you, your staff, the children and other users of your service.

Some of the equipment will have been installed in consultation with your architect at the planning stage and will be influenced by regulations within the building industry, as already discussed. There are specific standards outlined in the 2006 regulations in relation to:

- Security and access/boundaries/fences/signage.
- Floors and staircases.
- Windows and doors/locks/safe areas.
- Gas and electricity/wiring and cables.
- Machinery and equipment.
- Sleeping equipment and playpens.
- Seating equipment/storage/shelving/hooks.
- Safety gates.
- Sanitary equipment and provision.
- Chemical and effluent safety.
- Outdoor play areas.
- Animals.
- Outings.
- Smoking.
- Infectious diseases/preventive measures/procedures.

It is a requirement of the Child Care (Pre-School Services) (No. 2) (Amendment) Regulations 2006 that equipment in your setting is fit for purpose, non-toxic, in a proper state of repair and maintained in a clean and hygienic condition. Regulation 27 sets out the minimum standards that are required for all equipment. In the inspection tool mentioned above and available at www.hse.ie you will see the checklists for all equipment to determine if it complies with safety standards. You could use this as a guide in your quality assurance for all equipment in your setting. The key to maintaining the equipment at its best is to examine it regularly and make sure that any maintenance issues are dealt with in a timely manner, but also that you buy appropriate equipment (with required CE, Lion Mark, British Safety Authority Mark, Age Mark and Irish Design Quality Mark) in the first place.

The type of equipment you choose for your setting can also be determined by the processes you are going to follow in the care of the children. Equipment for Highscope, Montessori or Steiner will be chosen in accordance with the suggestions, layout and standards set by the philosophy being followed.

In relation to equipment for children, the list in the HSE inspection tool is a good starting point for anybody setting up a pre-school service.

0–1 year (approx.):

Natural materials	Hand-held toys
Treasure basket	Mirror
Sound-making toys	Sheltered outdoor area
Activity centres	Rattles
Insert shapes	Play mat
Cuddly toys	Pop-up toys
Puppets	Stackable bricks
Family photos/album	Softballs
Blow bubbles	Picture books
Tapes/CDs	
Mobiles	
Play bricks	

1–2½ years (approx.)

Natural materials	Tapes/CDs
Treasure basket	Play tea set
Water play	Playhouse
Musical toys/instruments	Chunky crayons
Toy kitchen	Paper dolls
Play phone	Cuddly toys
Duplo/stickle bricks	Pull/push toys
Family photos/album	Outdoor play area
Dressing-up clothes	Ride-on toys
Chunky hand-held toys	Sand play
Slides	Sound-making toys
Bubbles	Story
Play dough	Music videos

Toy foods   Puppets
Puzzles   Balls
Picture books   Climbing equipment

2½–6 years (approx.)

Nature and sensory: Slides/swings/seesaws
Natural materials   Nature display
Sand play   Water play
                                   Planting area/pots
Creative: Farm/animal toys
Paints   Play dough/shapes
Crayons   Cut and paste
Paper   Collage materials
Children's artwork/displays   Blackboard/chalk
                                   Tea set
Imaginative: Household objects
Toy kitchen   Clothes for dressing up
Playhouse   Quiet/reading area
Dolls   Puppets
Cots   Bricks/Lego/Duplo
Interest areas (shop/workbench/other)   Threading
                                   Pegging matching games
Language: Telephone
Books   Push toys/prams
Story   Puppets
Music videos   Tapes/CDs
                                   Wall posters
Manipulative (fine motor) and reasoning: Shape sorters
Stackable bricks   Jigsaws
Twisty toys   Free-running indoor/outdoor space
Puzzles   Balls
                                   Hoops
Physical (gross motor):   Jumping sacks
Dance music   Balancing beams
Ride-on toys   Climbing
Skittles   Bouncing equipment

Source: HSE inspection tool (www.hse.ie).

This is not an exhaustive list and there are many variations on the equipment you put into your setting, which will ultimately be determined by you and your staff. This will be based on the image you have of your own establishment as well as the type of service you want to offer and the ability needs of the children, parents and staff. Technology is not mentioned in the above list but is very much part of the modern child's life, whether we like it or not. Toys have a multiplicity of uses and each use should be taken into account when choosing equipment for your setting. Every facet of equipment must be considered when planning your service and the use of resources in the setting.

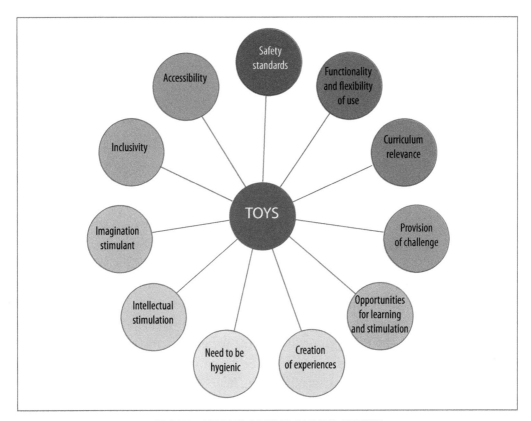

FIGURE 4.1: THE MULTIFUNCTIONAL ASPECTS OF TOYS IN YOUR SETTING

Reflective Portfolio Activity
Use the inspection tool on www.hse.ie to draw up a checklist for your setting to ensure compliance with the requirements under Regulation 27 of the Child Care (Pre-School Services) (No. 2) (Amendment) Regulations 2006 for the toys on your premises.

As part of this exercise, draw up a timetable to ensure that toys are examined and cleaned within the requirements of the HSE inspection criteria and make suggestions for any improvements you feel might be needed.

Remember, this exercise is for your own portfolio and is a reflective exercise. It is not meant to be a tool with which to criticise your placement. It is intended to give you focus for when you are in charge of this process in this or any other setting.

Planning

Any business must prepare a robust business plan if it is going to succeed. The purpose of the plan is to know exactly what is needed to fund, run and grow the business. A business plan is usually written with at least a three-year timescale. There are many people, such as accountants, consultants and bankers, who will help you prepare a business plan, but one of the best pieces of advice you will ever get is to become involved in the process yourself. By becoming familiar with the figures in your business plan, you will be able to work towards making sure that the things you want to prioritise can be included in the figures you produce. If you understand every piece of your plan, you will fully understand how to make it happen. For instance, there is no point asking a bank manager for an overdraft of €10,000 if what is really needed is €20,000.

Templates for business plans can be downloaded from many sources, such as enterprise boards, banks and money budgeting services. By their very nature, such templates are flexible and many require more detail than you may need to put into your plan, but you should use only enough to tell your story. For people who have never written a business plan they can be a chore, but getting involved in the process means that you know how to go about budgeting to meet the predictions you make in the process.

A simple business plan tells the story of the vision you have for your business and then translates the aspects of that vision into the financial requirements needed to make it happen. At all stages, if some part of the vision depicted in the plan does not have a figure to match it in the business plan, you are missing something and need to review the plan. Likewise, if there is a figure in the financial information that does not match a description in the written part of the business plan, an explanation of the amount should be put into the plan.

A simple business plan has several sections which, when read in the final version, state what exactly is envisaged.

The basics of a business plan

Executive Summary

This section usually succinctly summarises things in one page and encourages the reader to delve further. This is typically written last and inserted at the beginning, as it is a synopsis of the idea being proposed.

Introduction

This explains how the idea came about and why you think it will work. It could be where you explain that there is no other pre-school service in a four-mile radius or whatever compelling reason why you think this service would be worth opening.

The Proposal

This outlines what you intend to spend and how you view the service you will be offering. Things such as location, space, equipment, staffing, organisation and services should be included here. How will you organise everything that needs to be included in this section? The reader wants to understand everything about the potential business being proposed.

Marketing Plan

- You should describe the market as it exists and in doing so make a comparison with the existing or potential competition so that you can assure the reader that you will be able to survive even if there is competition.
- You should include a SWOT analysis in this part of the plan – a list of strengths, weaknesses, opportunities and threats. The reason this is included is similar to your own strengths analysis – to show how you expect to use opportunities or strengths to the advantage of the business and how you will minimise the effects of weaknesses or threats on your business by using other means or by making them work for you.
- Next you should describe who your users will be, what they would be willing to pay and how you propose to get business.
- In this section you should also say how you propose to market your service and what costs will be involved.
- You should also include the four Ps:
  - ▸ Price – how much you will charge and why.
  - ▸ Product – what you will or will not include.
  - ▸ Promotion – how you will advertise it.
  - ▸ Place – where in the market you will place your product, e.g. luxury, middle of the road or other.

The Financial Plan

This sets out how you propose to pay for everything in your vision and puts a price on the service you will offer as well as dealing with how you might be able to pay back the person who will support your vision. It will clearly say how your income will be generated and what you will have to pay out in expenses, as this allows whoever is reading the plan to see how you will make a profit or how you will support the service you are proposing to offer.

The financial plan should consist of at least the following:

● An income and expenditure statement.
● A profit and loss account.
● A balance sheet.

Remember, you will have to predict figures for at least three years, so you must be informed about likely trends in the next few years.

Summary

This allows you to put in anything extra that might make the vision more realistic for the reader. It also gives you another opportunity to summarise some aspects of each section in order to convince the reader.

Remember that everything you put into the picture needs to be in the business plan and should have a corresponding entry in the financial projections and vice versa. If you follow the guide you should not leave anything out, or you will then have to fund it from a different source – it is not good practice to go back to a bank manager and say you forgot to put in something and need more money before you even open!

Income and expenditure account

The following is a simple example of an income and expenditure account, which if accompanied by the relevant explanations for each figure in the text would be a good start to your business plan.

	Jan	Feb	Mar	Apr	May	Total
Income/cash inflow						
Bank loan	60,000	0	0	0	0	60,000
Owner's investment	10,000	0	0	0	0	10,000
Grants	5,000	0	0	0	0	5,000
Fees from baby room	0	0	4,800	4,800	4,800	14,400
Fees from toddler room	0	0	4,800	4,800	4,800	14,400
Fees from wobbler room	0	0	3,400	3,800	3,800	11,000
Fees from Montessori	0	0	3,000	3,000	3,000	9,000
Total cash inflow	75,000	0	16,000	16,400	16,400	123,800

continued	Jan	Feb	Mar	Apr	May	Total
Expenditure/cash outflows						
Staff wages	3,000	3,000	3,000	3,000	3,000	15,000
Employer's PRSI	450	450	450	450	450	2,250
Food	280	290	300	320	280	1,470
Set-up costs	1,300	0	0		0	1,300
Legal fees	500	0	0	0	0	500
Audit fees	200	100	100	100	100	600
Stamp duty	10	0	0	0	0	10
Repairs and maintenance	175	0	0	0	0	175
Light	40	25	25	25	18	133
Heat	45	45	30	30	30	180
Waste charges	40	40	40	40	40	200
Rates and/or rent	200	200	200	200	200	1,000
Bank fees	10	10	10	10	10	50
Loan repayments	790	790	790	790	790	3,950
Advertising	300	300	300	300	300	1,500
Cleaning	80	80	80	80	80	400
Administration	150	150	150	150	150	750
Training	100	100	100	100	0	400
Telephone	34	20	20	20	20	114
Insurance	200	200	200	200	200	1,000
Travel/motor	50	40	40	40	40	210
Subscriptions	100	0	0	0	0	100
HSE and other fees	280	0	0	0	0	280
TV licence	160	0	0	0	0	160
Art and craft materials	200	200	200	200	200	1,000
Staff uniforms	500	0	0	0	0	500
Total expenditure	9,194	6,040	6,035	6,055	5,908	33,232
Excess of income/expenditure	65,806	−6,040	9,965	10,345	10,492	90,568
Opening bank balance	60,000	125,806	119,766	129,731	140,076	
Excess of income/expenditure	65,806	−6,040	9,965	10,345	10,492	
Closing bank balance	125,806	119,766	129,731	140,076	150,568	

FIGURE 4.2: INCOME AND EXPENDITURE ACCOUNT, 31 MAY

There are some basic charges included in this example so that you can see the type of detail that should be included in your plan. Bin charges and other local charges must be factored into your business plan so that you can gauge how much your expenses will amount to.

You will also see that the example above has a presumed balance in the bank at the beginning to which any surplus of income over expenditure is added, giving a new bank balance figure at the end of the month. Over the period, watch how the bank balance is affected by what happens in the business. There are times when it is overdrawn and the reason you would predict this amount over the three-year period is so that you can see what your overdraft would need to be to match the most indebted month (on the basis that you get one finance package to start with and it is based on the three-year projections).

Reflective Portfolio Activity

Draw up an income and expenditure account for one year for a Montessori sessional service using the following details to start off.

Bank loan	€4,000
Owner's investment	€3,000

Currently there are 13 children in the Montessori class and they pay €100 per week for the service you offer from 9 a.m. to 12 p.m. daily. You pay €200 per week for the premises you rent.

Explain your reasons why each expense is at the level you put it at and show what the bank balance is each month.

Give suggestions as to how the service could make more money (e.g. by changing some details or cutting down expenses).

Profit and loss account

This is similar to the income and expenditure account, except it includes things you have not fully paid for. The income and expenditure account records exactly what was paid, while the profit and loss account records what should have been paid. For instance, you might have incurred an expense that does not have to be paid for until a month later (e.g. electricity or a credit card), so it would not appear in the income and expenditure as a payout but would appear in the profit and loss account as a cost that has been incurred. The purpose of the profit and loss account is to see how profitable the business is at any given time and it does this by taking into account expenses that have not yet been paid but still relate to the level of business done to that date.

Take a look at the profit and loss statement that would accompany the income and expenditure account given above.

	Jan	Feb	Mar	Apr	May	Total
Sales	0	0	16,000	16,400	16,400	48,800
Less cost of sales						
Wage costs	3,450	3,450	3,450	3,450	3,450	17,250
Food	280	290	300	320	280	1,470
Total cost of sales	3,730	3,740	3,750	3,770	3,730	18,720
Gross profit	−3,730	−3,740	12,250	12,630	12,670	30,080
Overheads						
Set-up costs	1,300	0	0	0	0	1,300
Legal fees	500	0	0	0	0	500
Audit fees	200	100	100	100	100	600
Stamp duty	10	0	0	0	0	10
Repairs and maintenance	175	0	0	0	0	175
Light	40	25	25	25	0	115
Heat	45	45	30	30	0	150
Waste charges	40	40	40	40	40	200
Rates and/or rent	200	200	200	200	200	1,000
Bank fees	10	10	10	10	10	50
Advertising	300	300	300	300	300	1,500
Cleaning	80	80	80	80	80	400
Admininstration	150	150	150	150	150	750
Training	100	100	100	100	0	400
Telephone	34	20	20	20	20	114
Insurance	200	200	200	200	200	1,000
Travel/motor	50	40	40	40	40	210
Subscriptions	100	0	0	0	0	100
HSE and other fees	280	0	0	0	0	280
TV licence	160	0	0	0	0	160
Art and craft materials	200	200	200	200	200	1,000
Staff uniforms	500	0	0	0	0	500
Total overheads	4,674	1,510	1,495	1,495	1,340	10,514
Net profit	−8,404	−5,250	10,755	11,135	11,330	19,566

FIGURE 4.3: PROFIT AND LOSS ACCOUNT AT 31 MAY

You should be able to see slight differences in the figures used in the two examples, which are about pre-payments or under-payments of expenses incurred in running the proposed business.

Balance sheet

Now take a look at the balance sheet. Notice that the amounts in the balance sheet for the figures that differed between the income and expenditure account and the profit and loss account are included in the balance sheet as an asset (something of worth to you) or a liability (something you owe).

Current assets			
Cash on hand			150,568
			150,568
Current liabilities			
Sundry creditors			48
			150,616
Represented by			
Capital introduced:			
Proprietor's cash	10,000		
Loans	120,000		
Grants	5,000	135,000	
Less loan repayments		3,950	131,050
Gross profit account			
Balance brought forward	0		
Add profit this year	19,566		19,566
			150,616

FIGURE 4.4: BALANCE SHEET AT 31 MAY

The difference between the three elements of the financial statements in a simple business start-up are as follows:

- Income and expenditure: What you actually received in and spent out.
- Profit and loss account: What you should have received in or spent out.
- Balance sheet: The difference.

Owning the business plan

As already mentioned, there are other ways of getting into business than setting up from scratch. As a supervisor, if you have taken over an existing position in a service that is already up and running, you should familiarise yourself with all of the above aspects in order to understand the dynamics of the business. You should carry out a strategic management process whenever you start in your supervisor capacity so that you know how things happen in the setting, why they happen that way and what changes could be made to achieve a more efficient service that best meets the needs of the service users.

Just as a business plan is a working document that should be re-examined regularly to see if it is working or needs review, you should look at every aspect of your service to ensure that the plan becomes part and parcel of how things are done to reach your goals. Build in regular reviews to look at what changes need to be made to ensure that your service is keeping up with your expectations. The secret of good business planning is constant engagement with the dynamics of the business so that the effect of any changes can be anticipated and provided for.

Resources

A resource is something that is of use to you in whatever you do. As a supervisor, you must have all the resources required to meet the needs of your service. The effective use or deployment of resources in your setting is fundamental to ensuring you achieve the breadth and depth of the vision you have for your setting. Getting things done is about using your resources to their best advantage, which requires you to know and understand exactly which resources you can use and how.

The pre-school setting is such a dynamic setting that the use of resources is almost endless if carefully planned. We have already seen how dynamic a child is and how all-encompassing the job of the supervisor is. Resourcefulness is about taking this type of approach to all the resources you have at the times you need to use them.

Money is one resource and is often the first one people think about, but this often has a finite limit to it (sometimes set by the banks in the form of an overdraft or loan), which requires you to budget and make careful use of it. However, money is not the only resource that can be of value to you in your pre-school setting. Other resources include:

TABLE 4.7

Staff	Adaptability Specialist training Shift hours Ideas Imagination	First aid training Languages Sense of humour Enthusiasm Connections, etc.
Your setting	Surroundings Area Community involvement Leisure facilities	Equipment _____ _____ _____
Finances	Overdrafts Credit cards Loans	Mortgages _____ _____
Parents	Support Involvement Skills Ideas and connections Loyalty	_____ _____ _____
You	Flexibility Foresight Network Other experiences Determination, etc.	_____ _____ _____ _____ _____

Fill in some resources in the lists above and explain your choices.

Reflective Portfolio Activity
Write a list of the resources you would bring to the job of supervisor in a crèche setting. In relation to five of these resources, write a paragraph on each to explain how they can be put to best use in the setting.

Budgeting

Budgeting is about getting what you need, when you need it, with the resources you have and being able to predict the needs that might arise and how they might be satisfied. In the income and expenditure account example above, budgeting would ensure that expenditure will at the very least match and never exceed income at any given time. The business plan is an important part of a budgeting process, as it sets out the likely sources of income and amounts of expenditure and shows what you expect to pay for a particular service over the time of the business plan projections. These figures become the budget you will work within, which is why it is so important that everything that you can possibly predict is in your business plan. There will always be some things you cannot predict, but when the unexpected happens, the money required must come from somewhere else, i.e. by cutting down on something else or generating more income somehow.

As a supervisor, you will be responsible for the careful budgeting of resources for your setting and therefore need to understand how the financial projections are worked out, as this allows you to be flexible when an unexpected expense arises. All staff should be aware that all business works to budgets, just as any country does. When all staff understand the limits of budgets, they learn how to create opportunities within the budget and should be encouraged to be resourceful in doing so. Good leaders allow their staff to become involved in the process: the staff on the ground are often the ones who know how savings can be made or additional income generated.

TABLE 4.8

Advantages of budgets	Disadvantages of budgets
<ul><li>They allow logical and predictable planning within the financial plan.</li><li>They create a picture of the financial position in a business at any point in time.</li><li>They allow staff to understand the monetary implications of their activities.</li><li>They help maintain records in an orderly and easy-to-understand fashion.</li></ul>	<ul><li>They can be rigid and limiting if they do not allow for fluctuations.</li><li>They can be time-consuming to generate in the first place.</li><li>They may frighten people who do not understand how they work.</li><li>They may limit the activities in the setting.</li></ul>

Like them or hate them, budgets are very much a part of every ECCE setting. When operated carefully they offer stability, a framework and confidence in the service's continuity.

Reflective Portfolio Activity

From the projections you did for your earlier portfolio activity, draw up a budget for expenses in your chosen setting. Show how one expense changing in the budget might have a knock-on effect on another expense, e.g. marketing might affect turnover.

Write a paragraph on how important it is to understand and know the budget for the activities in your setting and how they might impact on the activities of your setting.

Time Management

Time is a valuable resource in any business and effective time management is important in the seamless running of an ECCE setting. Children have schedules such as mealtimes, sleep times and going home times, to mention just a few. Managing everything within the day of each child and setting takes time management skills.

Budgeting time in the day is an important activity for such a valuable but limited resource and any supervisor will try to ensure that this resource is budgeted for carefully in order to get everything done. There are only 24 hours (1,440 minutes) in every day and as individuals we are not often aware of exactly how we use those hours. Yes, we all have different sleep requirements and because everybody is an individual we use time differently. However, a supervisor must look at how time is managed so that the resource is used to its best effect. The following portfolio activity is your first step in learning to be a good time manager.

Reflective Portfolio Activity

Draw up a chart that divides a day from a presumed waking time of 6.00 a.m. until midnight, seven days a week, and is divided into half-hour segments.

TIME	Mon	Tues	Wed	Thurs	Fri	Sat	Sun
6.00 a.m.							
6.30 a.m.							
7.00 a.m.							

For every half hour of each day, mark in what you usually do. You can use colour coding so that work is red, watching TV is blue, yellow is for socialising, purple is for free time, etc. Be truthful in this process until every box is filled in.

Now look realistically at what you do with your time every week. Are there wasted time slots? Are you on social networks for hours at a time (be truthful)? Do you get up later than you could?

Are there changes you could make that would make your life easier and less stressed and allow you extra study time that you did not realise you had?

What do you think would be the effect of making some small changes to your time management habits?

There will always be time you can allocate to leisure and other activities, but you might not be aware this time exists until you do an exercise like this. This type of time management chart should become one of your working tools for the future in your position as a supervisor. You could have one for each staff member, each grouping in the ECCE setting or some other category of your own making, as long as you understand it and can work with it. It is a tool that allows you to realistically determine what budget changes you can make with the resource of time to ensure that you work efficiently within the budget given. You could use colour coding, for example, to allocate opening and closing times to particular staff. Or you might notice that some groups of children work best if they do art at a particular time of the day, so the chart could allow you to slot in a time for this activity so that the children get the best from their energy levels; or you could focus on whatever priorities you wish to set. Using this type of time management tool puts you in charge of the way the time is used.

Treating time like a resource that should not be wasted will allow you to see opportunities where you can multitask and put systems in place to undertake tasks in your ECCE setting efficiently. Nowadays all computers, laptops, hand-held devices, mobile phones and some standalone devices have timetables and charts that you can utilise for effective time management: they often come with to do lists (computers even have sticky notes that stay on the screen until the activity is marked as complete).

All you need to do is find the system or device that works best for you and start to implement it as soon as you can – you will be surprised how quickly you learn which one suits you best and how much of a difference it makes to your methods of getting things done. Set aside a time every day to do your timetable or to do list and this will become an effective habit.

You might find that you think more clearly in the morning and/or you might like to set aside a half hour after work when you can think clearly. Phone calls could be grouped together every day so that they take less time. Nobody can tell you which system suits you best and you must find the one that works for you. In this process you can refer to your reflective journal to see what has worked well in the past. Remember to use technology if you have it – there are many different programs that you can try until you find the one that works for you – or a simple written diary might be your preferred method. Running around like a headless chicken is stressful, and that is what happens if you do not learn a system of time management that works for you, your staff and your setting.

FIVE

Consultation in the ECCE Setting

I t is important for any supervisor to understand the processes outlined in Chapter 4. It will help you know enough about your setting to see how everything interacts as well as appreciate that every change you make in the setting can have an impact on something else. It also allows you to acknowledge how dynamic and interrelated all aspects of an ECCE setting are. Whether you understand this process through setting up your own service or by being familiar with the details of a setting in which you are employed, there is no substitute for the understanding that comes from knowing the processes from the very basics up.

Mission Statement

When envisaging the idea for a pre-school service and going through the process of writing a business plan, you have a concept of what your service will be like. In this process, you define the mission of your service, and this will become the beginning of your mission statement.

A mission statement puts your idea for your setting, its reason for being, how it interacts with others and its goals into a written format that is a descriptive and inspiring commitment to making it happen. It is a succinct statement (about six sentences) that is to the point, believable, achievable and focused on the ideals and uniqueness of your service. As the mission statement is often used in advertising and promoting your service, care should be taken to ensure that the words used in the mission statement do not lead to legal expectations that might not be fulfilled (e.g. saying all children will be catered for when only 12 could possibly fit into the setting).

In essence, a mission statement is a written formula. It is useful to start the process with the 5 Ws + 1H of writing – the who, why, where, when, what and how:

- **What** do you see as the goal, vision, aim or mission of the service?
- **Why** is this of relevance to you or the children, parents or others who work in or for the service?
- **Who** is likely to benefit from this service?
- **How** are they likely to benefit?
- **Where** will it make a difference to them?
- **When** will it make this difference?

Using a word bank as a starting point helps to get the process of writing the statement started, but they are no substitute for your personal description. A thesaurus is useful, as it lists words that have similar meanings and can help you choose the best words for the job.

Reflective Portfolio Activity

Write a six-sentence mission statement for the service you have outlined in your sample business plan from Chapter 4. As part of this exercise, use the following word bank or find appropriate words for your vision in a thesaurus.

commitment	ethos
envisage	needs
endeavour	children
aim	parents
mission	partnerships
vision	involving
goal	open
concept	environment
growth	inclusive
potential	culture
ideal	ethnicity
concept	race
explore	equality
challenge	philosophy
relationship	

Never underestimate the power of your mission statement. It should direct the ethos of the setting, and even more important, it should instil a sense of belonging and commitment from all who work in, visit and use the service.

Just as your business plan is a working document, so too is your mission statement, as it is likely to change over time and should be regularly revisited to check that it is still relevant to the workings of the service. It is such a pivotal piece of writing that it is a task that is best produced in consultation with others who can question and examine the meaning and implications of every word used. Staff should be fully versed in the process, as part of their work is to make sure that the goals stated are clearly understood and are implemented.

You can look at phrases used in other mission statements, but you should not be overly influenced by what you read, as this is a personal process that should be undertaken in consultation with the people who will be expected to implement it, those who will be affected by it and those who can contribute to its implementation – in other words, the stakeholders in the service.

Stakeholders

A stakeholder is anybody who is affected by the service you operate or the way in which you operate that service. While the people who own the service may be shareholders, i.e. they own part of the business, the stakeholders may have no actual ownership of the business but either give or get something from its operation, as depicted in Figure 5.1.

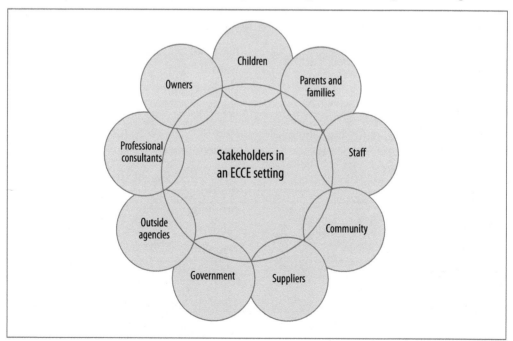

FIGURE 5.1: STAKEHOLDERS IN AN ECCE SETTING

Reflective Portfolio Activity

For each of the stakeholders listed in Figure 5.1, say how they either affect or are affected by the service you have described in your business plan above

TABLE 5.1

Stakeholder	Affects ECCE setting	Affected by ECCE setting
Children		
Parents and families		
Staff		
Community		
Suppliers		
Government		
Outside agencies		
Professional consultants		
Owners		

Rank the stakeholders from 1 to 9, with 9 being the stakeholder who is most influenced by the way the ECCE setting is run on a daily basis.

Depending on the type of ECCE service you operate, there will be a number of stakeholders, including children and their parents, who have a direct involvement in how the ECCE setting operates. Other stakeholders, such as professional consultants and the community, are not as involved on a daily basis and thus have an indirect involvement. When drawing up your mission statement, the stakeholders who are directly involved in your service should be consulted and be fully committed to the project, as they will be a direct part of making it happen. Indirect stakeholders should also be considered, as what you do will have an impact on them, e.g. a window cleaner gains income from the service for cleaning the windows but does not have a direct effect on how the service operates.

Keeping Stakeholders Informed

Stakeholders, whether direct or indirect, need to be kept informed about what is happening in the setting because they have an interest in what is going on. There should be open communication with all involved, which you as a supervisor should initiate, support and sustain. A simple example would be where the window cleaner comes every week on a Tuesday but the ECCE setting proposes to close for some reason on one particular Tuesday next month. In this case, it makes sense to inform the window cleaner when the setting will be closed, as this facilitates the window cleaner's planning and does not incur a charge for the window cleaner's time.

Information is a way of giving all stakeholders a sense of belonging, especially for children and parents, so there should be constant communication with these stakeholders. In such cases, information needs to be communicated as a two-way process so that questions and answers flow both ways (methods of initiating such communication will be covered in Chapter 14). As a supervisor, you should identify all the stakeholders in your setting and observe what constraints exist and what preferences stakeholders have in relation to the way they receive information. Getting information to people efficiently must happen within the budget of the setting and you need to look carefully at the ways in which you communicate information. Colourful displays, letters, newsletters, etc. may suffice, but you should match the method to the needs (for instance, a display of all staff members with their relevant qualifications can be very reassuring for parents). In this regard, and in relation to your mission statement, you should consider whether information needs to be translated into all the different languages that are represented in your setting.

Being aware of all your setting's stakeholders will mean that you consider the implications of your decisions for them and how you can incorporate policies in your setting in order to ensure that their views are asked for, questions answered and worries eased. This will make for a secure, well-supported and smooth-running environment for all those in the setting, but most important, for the children in your care.

> *Reflective Portfolio Activity*
> Examine the ways in which your setting communicates with and keeps three different stakeholders in the setting informed. Write a paragraph on why you think the methods used do or do not do the job well. What would you change if you were the supervisor of the setting?

Equality

Equality is at the very essence of our Constitution and is a fundamental right of every person in this country. The Employment Equality Acts 1998 and 2004 and the Equal Status Acts 2000–2004 clearly set out the law in Ireland in relation to:

- Equality of pay for equal work.
- Equality of opportunity for promotion, training or information.
- An individual's right not to be discriminated against on nine specific grounds.

The nine grounds of discrimination are:
1. Travellers: Travellers should never be discriminated against on the grounds of their membership of the Travelling community.
2. Race: Belonging to a particular race of people should not mean that you are treated unequally.
3. Religion: Whatever your religion is, it should not be a source of discrimination.
4. Age: Under-18s are not included on this age ground and an exception is made in relation to car insurance for young people.
5. Marital status: Being married, divorced or separated should not lead to you being treated unequally.
6. Sexuality: This includes the fact that a person may be transgender.
7. Gender: This can include a woman being treated unfairly in relation to pregnancy issues that arise in the workplace.
8. Family status: Examples of family status are blended family, single parent, etc.
9. Disability: Having a recognised disability should not preclude you from participation.

A good mnemonic for remembering these nine grounds of discrimination is: **TRRAMS** are **G**ood **F**or **D**ublin.

It is against the law for anybody to be discriminated against on the above grounds. Discrimination is described as when a person is 'treated less favourably than another person is, has been or would be treated in a comparable situation' (Equality Act 2004). Equality is not an option but an absolute requirement in any workplace.

The *Diversity and Equality Guidelines for Childcare Providers*, published as part of the National Childcare Strategy 2006–2010, which can be downloaded as a PDF at www.dcya.gov.ie, is a resource you should be familiar with when undertaking an equality audit of your setting. These guidelines will help you to examine the impact of all your actions in the quest for equality in any setting and you should read them in conjunction with an examination of your own setting's practices. The guidelines define equality as 'the importance of recognising different individual needs and of ensuring equity in terms of access, participation and benefits for all children and their families. It is therefore not about treating people the "same".'

In childcare, therefore, where a child needs extra resources to achieve the same as another child, they should be facilitated so that they will reach their best potential. Staff and systems must be willing to change as the need arises in relation to individual children.

The most important proponent of equality in your setting is *you* – children, staff, parents and others will take their lead from you. If you take a proactive approach to any equality issues that arise in your setting, then all stakeholders will understand what the boundaries are. You must therefore always be aware of and constantly challenging your equality measures to ensure that they are robust. Equality should always be treated as a work in progress. As your setting adjusts (e.g. when new staff, children or parents come into the setting or when there are societal changes), you should equality-proof your systems to ensure that equality is achieved. Where the setting is found wanting, you should be prepared to take positive action and continually monitor the results.

By law, every workplace must deal with any equality issues that arise and every ECCE setting must have an equality policy that can be inspected, as set out in the Child Care (Pre-School Services) (No. 2) (Amendment) Regulations 2006. This requires you to look at every aspect of your service to make sure that people are being treated equally as well as taking measures to ensure that equality is understood and reflected in the ways people interact in your setting. There are implications for any service that does not confirm that equality is at the centre of what they do:

- Inefficiencies of work and responsibilities.
- Lack of esteem for the person who is being treated unequally.
- An ECCE setting is a care and education setting, so it is important to establish an expectation of equality in all children in your care so that they reach their full potential – inequality stifles achievement of potential.
- Possible expensive court challenges to your actions or legally imposed fines.
- Disputes, an unhappy workforce and time spent resolving disputes.
- Unhealthy environment for everybody, as inequality can cause stress and conflict.
- Lost publicity and marketing opportunities – there is nothing as powerful as a person who has a bad experience to relate, and parents often compare notes about childcare settings when choosing such care.
- Social impact of unhappiness on children and parents.
- High staff and child turnover as people choose other settings.
- Waste of talent and training as people are held back.

Whether you are taking over the supervision of an existing setting or starting up a new setting, you must tackle any equality issues that arise in your setting. You must carry out a comprehensive examination of the whole service and ensure that:

- Your recruitment, promotions, training and opportunities systems address any potential equality issues in the workplace.
- Your registration, selection and induction processes are open, clearly worded, transparent and equality sensitive.
- The operation of your service is such that equality issues are dealt with proactively and are promptly dealt with should they arise.
- The messages you send out to parents and other stakeholders include them in the process of instilling equality awareness in the setting.

- The children in your care are aware that they and others are equal and that your setting does not give any messages that could cause inequality, particularly in relation to images, posters, memos and other communication methods.
- All toys and resources in your setting are sensitive to any potential equality issues under any category.
- The example you give encourages equality in every aspect of your work and interactions.

Reflective Portfolio Activity

Look at your setting and identify 10 equality-positive initiatives.

- For each of the 10 initiatives, write a paragraph on how you consider it achieves or respects equality in the setting.
- Identify two actions that you would recommend to improve equality in the setting if you were the supervisor.

Please remember that this exercise is for your portfolio and that discretion should be maintained in relation to your setting.

Decision-making

Decision-making can be one of the most challenging aspects of your job as a supervisor, but it is one aspect of your work that will improve with practice and careful thought. Decision-making is about choosing from a range of solutions to a problem, evaluating the choice you make to find the best one for the situation that arises and implementing that decision.

There are several steps outlined in this process and each has its own dynamic.

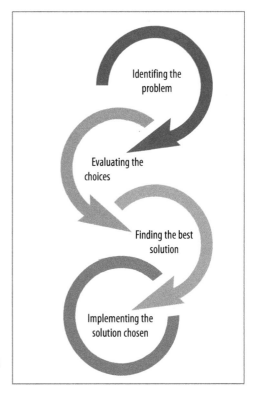

Identifying the problem

Evaluating the choices

Finding the best solution

Implementing the solution chosen

FIGURE 5.2: THE DECISION-MAKING PROCESS

Identifying the problem or challenge

This requires you to be aware of what is happening in your setting and have your information processes in place. You must be attuned to the possibility that problems may arise or already exist or that changes need to be implemented, and you must therefore be proactive in your examination of your setting and the environment in which you operate.

Factors that affect the identification process are:
- Procrastination – knowing change must be implemented but putting off the inevitable.
- Ignoring the signs – knowing something is not right but not being able to see exactly what it is or believing that it cannot happen in your setting.
- Outside forces could require you to make decisions, e.g. government or legislative changes.
- You may have a 'head in the sand' attitude to problems that arise.
- Lack of support for change.
- Misinformation – not exactly lies, but not the full truth on which to base your decision.

Evaluating the choices

This requires you to look at the possibilities you can choose from. This may be done in consultation with others or may be an individual process, which can be quicker than getting consensus from a team. However, choice should not be based solely on the need for speed, but should be a combination of all the influencing factors.

Factors that affect the evaluation process are:
- Some steps may already be set out in the setting's policies.
- Advice you may receive from somebody who has already faced a similar situation.
- Who is most qualified to make the decision?
- The consequences of each possible course of action.
- Some choices may be forced upon you by circumstances, e.g. you may need to protect a child in immediate danger and must act in the child's best interests.
- Your choices may be based on the best information available at the time rather than all the information possible.

Finding the best solution

This may require you to take into account the circumstances that created the need for the decision in the first place, the person or people who will be affected by the decision and how your choice might impact on your setting.

Factors that affect the choice of the best solution are:

- Finding the best fit for everybody involved and your setting.
- Some decisions, though they are for the best, may make you feel ineffectual and this can prevent you from choosing them.
- Whether your solution is short term (if wrong, it is only for a short while) or a more permanent fix.
- Whether the solution is intuitive or takes more thought, including looking at the implications of your decisions.
- Whether the solution fits in with your plans for the setting going forward.
- There may be financial or other implications to your decision and you may need time to weigh these up.
- Knowing that some people will not be happy with your decision or, more specifically, with the impact your decision will have on them.

Implementing the solution you have chosen

Whether or not this is the first time you have made a significant decision in the running of your setting, you are likely to be conscious of how your decision will work out for everybody concerned. There will be times when people try to make you feel guilty for the decisions you make and times when everybody is happy with your decision – you must think of each as an experience that helps you grow in your role as supervisor or leader. If you use your reflective diary effectively in the decision-making process, you will have a resource for when a similar decision arises again.

Factors that can affect the implementation process are:

- Fear – get on with it and deal with it is the best approach here.
- Others may be disappointed. However, the same people will not be affected by every decision, so a balanced perspective is important.
- The decision may be a great success and you berate yourself for not making it sooner.
- You may indeed come to love the decision you make and will get better at making decisions in the future.

Remember, your job is to make a difference to all your stakeholders and you must be prepared in all instances to put the best interests of the child at the centre of everything you do. Those are the guidelines within which all your decisions should be made in your setting, whether as part of a team or on an individual basis. Practice is one of your best allies in the art of decision-making and you will get better over time. This is why you should also record your decisions and the criteria you used to make those decisions as part of your reflective journal and as part of a learning process.

Reflective Portfolio Activity
Write an account of when you had to make a decision in the daily work of your setting and explain the steps you took to make that decision. Discuss the difficulties you found while making the decision. Explain why you think the decision was effective and how it made a difference in the setting.

Networking

Networking is another form of maximising resources in the ECCE setting. This time the resource is you and your own knowledge, which should never be taken for granted. Networking is about creating connections with other people who can form part of a meaningful business relationship. These connections can be used to support your work and may become a sounding board when decisions need to be made in your setting. While individual connections can be made that are significant, networking allows you connect to more people than just your initial connection.

In Ireland we are very good at 'knowing somebody who knows somebody' and are therefore well versed in the art of networking without even realising it. If we have a problem, we usually see if we know somebody who has the skill to help us solve it. In any networking process, it is important to remember that you get as good as you give, so you must be prepared to invest time and effort in making your network effective for everybody concerned. When working efficiently you can support others, and receive support, as well as learning valuable lessons from other people's experiences.

Reasons why you should build a network include:

- Getting support for difficult decisions.
- It can help relieve stress and give a sense of camaraderie.
- Your network can become a sounding board for decisions you must make.
- Potential hazards or risks can be pointed out to you before you experience them.
- Your network may include people who have considerable experience in the industry and their experience can become a resource for you.
- Your contacts may have more up-to-date information about changes in the industry that you can benefit from.

Like your reflective diary, the network you create for yourself will expand and your level of input will increase over time and through experience. You should acknowledge that you may not be well informed as you start out, but you should continue to examine your sources and add to your network as you grow into your role.

Possible sources for your own network:
- Family and friends.
- Colleagues.
- Parents in the setting.
- Classmates you were at college with.
- Teachers and lecturers in college.
- Professional associations.
- City and county childcare committees.
- Online forums, which should be used with care and respect for confidentiality.
- Chambers of commerce.
- Voluntary organisations, e.g. ISPCC, Barnardos, Gingerbread.

A network will grow gradually as you and others add to the list of contacts you have. As you use the network, you will become more involved in any discussions that may take place.

Keeping Up to Date

It is imperative for your professional standing and the effectiveness of your position as supervisor, and indeed for the care and education of the children in your setting, that you keep up to date with developments in the ECCE sector. Keeping up to date allows your setting to function efficiently in an industry that has seen much change in recent years and is likely to continue to change as our population changes.

Reading and continuing professional development are fundamental parts of keeping informed about developments in childcare and this should be part of your reflective processes as a professional.

There are different categories of change that you must keep yourself informed about, such as:
- Legislation changes that may have implications in your setting.
- Staff training and qualifications changes.
- Industry changes and trends that may result in efficiencies in your setting.
- Social changes that can impact on parents, children or staff.
- Curriculum changes that need to be incorporated into your work, e.g. Aistear.
- Financial and tax changes that can impact on your recordkeeping and finances.

There will be some methods of keeping up to date that you will naturally prefer depending on how you like to get your information, and your network will form part of that process. Nowadays there are many sources of information and you may decide to partake of a number of sources, such as:

- Subscriptions to childcare organisations, which may include taking part in workshops.
- E-zines from industry and voluntary organisations.
- Newspapers.
- Industry magazines.
- Government-sponsored training events.
- City and county childcare committees.
- Websites of relevant organisations, such as www.naionrai.ie, www.ncna.ie, www.ispcc.ie and www.barnardos.ie.

Many of the organisations you subscribe to will have their own websites, newsletters and online e-zines, which are a great source of information to keep you up to date. The best way to keep yourself informed is to get involved in these organisations and be at the centre of what is happening, but failing that, make sure you have your systems and networks in place so that you hear about changes in the making.

Reflective Portfolio Activity
Sign up for three e-zines that will be of assistance to you in your job as supervisor and write a paragraph on each to explain how you feel it will help you in your role.

SIX

Interactions in the ECCE Setting

An ECCE setting is a dynamic, active, enabling and organised environment that works seamlessly if carefully managed. As we have seen, it is one where all stakeholders' interests should be considered when decisions are made.

Working with Parents/Carers

The most significant stakeholders are the children in the setting, who are effectively its reason for being. Parents make the decision as to what ECCE service to use based on their own criteria, but parents are not the end users of the service and staff act *in loco parentis* when caring for the children in the setting. However, this does not mean that staff members have absolute autonomy in the decisions they make for each child. Consultation with the parent, together with ongoing information and feedback, is the cornerstone of good childcare and education. Every child in Ireland is afforded the protection of the family and parents are the primary educators of the child under our Constitution – trust is therefore the basis of any childcare relationship and that trust requires interactions with parents and including them as partners in the child's care.

Partnership implies mutuality – a sense of working together towards one goal, which is the best possible care for the child in the setting. As supervisor, you are responsible for creating and overseeing the interaction systems in your setting, so this should be a constant focus if you are to create a happy, functioning and professional service in which children and their parents or guardians feel respected and included. This mutuality requires input from both parents and the setting.

TABLE 6.1

Parents bring	The setting brings
• Willingness to trust and an expectation that staff put the child at the centre of their work. • Expectations of expertise in childcare and education. • Knowledge of the child's likes and dislikes. • Family background and history. • Respect for the skills of childcare workers and the setting's standards. • Willingness to share information and reinforce the work of the setting.	• Trust that parents are open and honest in relation to their child's needs. • Expectations of an open and informative relationship with the parent/guardian. • Child development knowledge, theory and practice. • Expertise on how to work with the child to ensure that the child meets their best potential. • Respect for the special relationship that exists between a child and a parent/guardian. • Reassurance and positive attitude to the needs of the child and parent who may need extra support.

There are a number of factors that may affect the important relationship between parent/guardian and the setting, some of which include the following.

Life factors

Siblings, families, job stresses, poverty, mental health issues, lack of outside support, disability and illness are examples of life factors that may arise from time to time in people's lives. Emotional times in people's lives, such as times of bereavement or serious illness, can also affect their ability to cope.

Intimidation

Parents do not necessarily hold qualifications in childcare and may feel overwhelmed by the task, or indeed they may feel intimidated by the qualifications and experience of staff members in the setting. There may even be instances where other parents in the setting intimidate parents who are not overly confident or who feel under pressure.

Social factors

The recession and money stresses can leave parents in a vulnerable position. They may not have wider family support where they live due to the need to migrate from their family network for job or other reasons.

Educational factors

Not every parent has received a full education and some may have numeracy or literacy issues they do not wish to divulge but which may affect their ability to share information efficiently.

Cultural factors

Parents come from a wide variety of backgrounds and there may be a reluctance in their culture to engage with authority, perceived or otherwise. Parents might have cultural expectations that do not fit into the ethos of the setting or its mission. Language may also be a cultural factor that might intimidate parents in a setting.

The Supervisor's Role in Equality

As a supervisor, you are expected to put in place a system for each child that takes all of the above issues into account. The establishment of a key worker for each child is a way of ensuring that parents become familiar and comfortable with the people who interact with their child. As supervisor, you must select the best person for this role, balancing the abilities of the key worker and the needs of the child as well as the ability of the key worker to act as a liaison with the parents/guardians. That person may be you in some settings, but if not you, you must develop a system that promotes open and productive communication for all concerned.

The key worker's ability to liaise between the parents, the setting and the child is hugely important in the successful integration of the child in the setting, as is the ability to create an atmosphere in which the child can thrive while gaining the confidence, co-operation and support of the parents. This system is especially, but not exclusively, important where a child or indeed a parent has a disability or needs extra support, as happens from time to time in people's lives. Being receptive to the needs of everybody in your service, which involves tact and diplomacy from any supervisor, makes for a rewarding, proactive and settled environment. The rewards are enormous in the lives of all concerned, including you.

Approaches to Childcare

As we have seen, parents' choices play a significant part in the selection of the pre-school setting they choose for their child. While you would expect that some of the issues that influence the choice they make would include cost, proximity, size, work-fit, word-of-mouth recommendations, school location, etc., not every choice is about such practicalities. Some parents will spend time choosing the setting based on its approach to childcare and how it is implemented in the setting.

The choice of approach of your setting may be incorporated into your design of the setting, but much of its implementation will be obvious from the day-to-day organisation of the setting and this can have a significant influence on the setting chosen.

Example of approaches to childcare include the following.

Naoínraí

Naoínraí are unique to Ireland. All activities, signage and interactions are through the medium of Irish. This has become more popular in recent years since the Irish language was recognised as an official EU language. This is an example of a **culture-led setting** where the customs, language, games and traditions of the children are obvious in the daily routines, etc.

Montessori

Maria Montessori, an Italian doctor working with children with disabilities, devised a system of education that used set pieces of didactic materials, which encouraged children to learn independently while encouraging dexterity through using the materials. The setting has a structured set-up and the materials are displayed in a way that encourages a child to interact with them when they are ready. This is an example of a **materials-led setting** where children learn in a structured and methodical manner and play is not the centre of focus.

Steiner

Rudolf Steiner believed that the child's temperament is paramount and that young children under the age of seven should be nurtured through diet, rest and interactions that are supportive of a young child. Toys are specific and community involvement in the setting is a big part of the ethos of the setting. This is an example of an **inclusive community setting** where everybody becomes part of the Steiner community that supports the child.

Froebel

Frederick Froebel, the founder of kindergarten, believed that children should be physically active and free to move and play and that much learning takes place through the medium of play and imagination. Special toys or gifts are a source of imagination for the children and the arts, music and interactions between children are valued. This type of **interpretive setting** encourages children to stretch their thinking through imagination.

Applied behaviour analysis (ABA)

ABA is concerned with behaviour adjustment, focusing on positives, and in Ireland is mostly concerned with children in the autism spectrum. It concentrates on behaviours that have social significance and observes behavioural changes encouraged by the method until they become stable and are eliminated or adapted. Because of the high degree of observation involved in this **behaviour-based setting**, there is a low child/adult ratio to ensure that the child gets the best out of the process.

Reggio Emilia

Developed after World War II, this is a setting that is based on Italian traditions. It concentrates on family and community involvement, as would be traditional in Italy. Teachers are learners and children undertake projects that can take any direction in pursuit of learning. The outdoor environment is an important source of learning for children. When finished, their projects are displayed with narratives as to how they changed and grew into projects, which can be revisited by groups of children who wish to add to the knowledge created. This is very much a **project, observation and wonder-based setting** with staff watching the children to see where the learning will go and what peers will be involved at each stage. The layout supports the openness of the outdoors, work areas and displays as well as parental involvement in the process.

High Scope

This is a type of setting that allows the child to decide what they want to learn. All materials are at child height and accessible. The adult supports and encourages the child once they have made their choice by enabling them to create goals and challenges in their learning. This is an **enabling setting** as the child decides the activity and carries it out under supervision rather than instruction.

Aistear

An Aistear setting is one that is **curriculum-led**. Examples of curriculum activity are included in the handbook for practitioners. It is a setting that will support children in their school curriculum over time. All activities and resources are seen as being capable of implementation into the curriculum as methods of learning and practitioners are encouraged to be adaptive in their approach to opportunities for learning.

Summary

All these approaches have their own following and parents will pick the setting which best fits their idea of childcare and early education or the needs of the child. The setting will have different layouts, colour schemes, interactions, projects, equipment and staff training based on the approach adopted. There is a move, through Aistear and its implementation, to incorporate many of these approaches into all ECCE settings in the form of an adaptive curriculum framework, with all abilities being catered for. However, parents will seek out options for their child based on their own criteria, and as supervisor you need to be consistent in creating an environment that reflects the chosen approach and encourages all children in your care to reach their best potential. Parents need to understand just what to expect when they engage with your setting and to know what to expect in their interactions with the setting. Ensuring that your interactions and those of your staff are informative, consistent with the stated mission statement of the setting, consistent with the chosen approach of the setting, respectful of the individuality of each child in the setting and the wishes and needs of the parents will mean that informed choices are possible for parents.

Child-centred Interactions

One of the most important aspects of your work as a supervisor is the facilitation of every child to reach their best potential, as outlined in the UNCRC (see Chapter 3). Additionally, you have a responsibility to create a setting that allows children to engage with the setting in a manner that is consistent with their needs. Interactions must be facilitated that are real and effective and make the child feel a valued and respected member of your setting.

Article 13 of the UNCRC states:

> The child shall have the right to freedom of expression; this right shall include freedom to seek, receive and impart information and ideas of all kinds, regardless of frontiers either orally, in writing or print, in the form of art, or through any other media of the child's choice.

To uphold this right as supervisor, you need to examine the ways in which you and your staff engage with children and encourage them to participate in everyday life in the setting. While children learn primarily from their parents and peers, you play a very important part in creating the child's expectations for meaningful engagement in other settings throughout their lives. Children encounter many opportunities to interact in an ECCE setting. They interact with materials, curriculum, challenges, themselves, their peers, their key worker, other professionals in the setting, their community, you and their parents. These interactions need to be balanced according to the child's age and stage of development. It is easy to see a small baby's preferences, if one is observant, and to engage with toddlers or other pre-school children as they develop in your setting. All staff should be encouraged to work with children to improve their ability to interact and their confidence in doing so.

To facilitate effective interactions with children in your setting, you should ensure that the task is approached in a multifaceted way that is constantly reviewed as each child engages with your procedures so that your systems work for that particular child at that stage in their life. The system should be one where everything works smoothly, as the benefits to the child are enormous and are reflected in a happy setting where all children contribute to the process. If this process necessitates training for staff who will be working closely with a child with specific needs (e.g. learning sign language), you must oversee this process and encourage everybody in the setting to learn something about sign language so that interactions are facilitated across the whole setting.

As supervisor, you need to create times for such interactions and oversee your staff in creating opportunities for such interactions. This is an ongoing task and should be included as part of your time management so that you prioritise it. You should also seek opportunities to engage with individual children outside the timetabled activity, as it is not just about circle time, but about answering questions a child may have or allaying a worry they have.

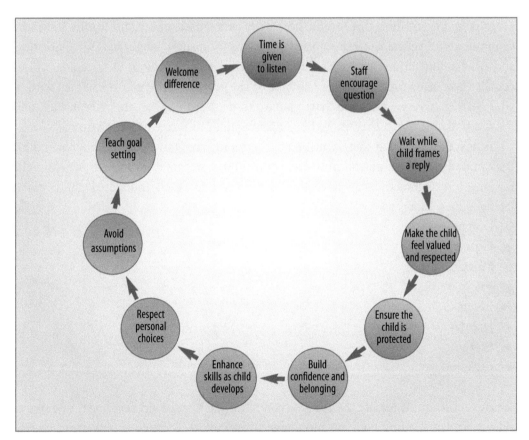

FIGURE 6.1: THE MEANING OF CHILD-CENTRED INTERACTIONS

> *Reflective Portfolio Activity*
> Over one week in your setting, note 10 interactions with children that take place across the age range and describe how they are dealt with. Explain how these interactions are received and whether you feel the children could gain more from the interaction and how.

Ethnicity

In an increasingly globalised world where people migrate for any number of reasons – torture, poverty, religion, economic necessity, suppression or even the pursuit of freedom – you can expect that they will bring some of their home culture with them. Ethnicity as we know it in childcare is about shared values, traditions, practices and beliefs that are based on where a person belongs or comes from. We have minority ethnic groupings in every country, and one that would be readily recognised in Ireland is the Travelling Community. Travellers share recognised traditions (nomadic), language (Cant), practices and beliefs and form a recognised and, as such, protected minority grouping in our equality laws. However, Travellers may not be the only minority group you deal with in your setting. Every child will have some ethnic features that are relevant to their background and which they should be encouraged to integrate into the setting.

In any ECCE setting there will be children and parents who have different ethnic backgrounds and each person must feel valued in the setting if they are to benefit while in your care. Ethnicity may have different aspects for each individual child and it includes such things as:

- Language
- Expressions
- Music
- Art
- Foods
- Holidays
- Clothing
- Customs

Whatever the ethnic feature the child or parent displays, it should never be the source of ridicule in your setting and you must make every effort to create an environment that facilitates the integration of ethnicity in the setting. This may mean openly challenging unfair or unjust practices by parents, staff, children and visitors.

Dealing with ethnicity positively and proactively is one of the best ways to ensure that the people who use your setting respect everybody, regardless of ethnic background. Discrimination often happens because children or others do not understand (not dislike or reject, but simply not understand) the elements of ethnicity for each person. Remember, each of us has an ethnic background; even individual counties in Ireland have differences in the ways they address festivals, foods and language. Your setting should encourage discussion on differences that explains that we all do things differently and should then use the difference in positive ways. Children may watch three ways of doing something and actually choose one of the new ways they see as being better for their own abilities or limitations. A positive way to address ethnicity would be to have an International Day where parents and children share the customs, sweets, foods and artefacts of each others' countries or you could introduce specific days for each ethnic background so that children learn from each other and from each others' parents; and they will be proud to show off and learn to appreciate their own culture. Your staff can help to organise this event and it would also be a source of in-house training for them.

Another method is simply observing different ways of doing things as they arise in the setting on a day-to-day basis, explaining the difference to enable everybody to understand and embrace it. Children should be encouraged to ask questions, experience differences and learn about their own ethnicity as part of their development – they may not want to replicate what they see, but they will want to understand and should be encouraged to learn.

Culture

Culture is closely aligned to the concept of ethnicity and is seen more clearly in the methods people use to express themselves. In Ireland we place great store on eye contact, but not every culture holds eye contact in such esteem and some actually discourage it.

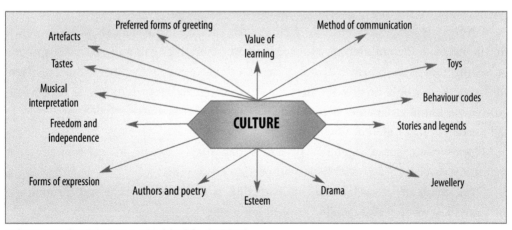

FIGURE 6.2: CULTURE IN A PRE-SCHOOL SETTING

Culture adds difference to interactions and can be seen in many situations in a pre-school setting. Learning about different cultures can be exciting for children, and like learning about ethnicity it encourages positive interactions with difference, which is a fundamental part of a child's life. Encouraging interactions takes time, thought, sensitivity and foresight on the part of any supervisor, but you are duty bound to ensure that children understand their own culture and can engage with others from different cultures. In all your planning for activities, you should include culture in any child-centred interactions and this should be reviewed regularly. Whenever a child joins your setting you should have enough information through your application forms, interactions with the child and parents/guardians and the assigned key worker to understand what you may need to incorporate into the setting. Every child should feel proud of their culture and your setting, if sensitively prepared, can contribute to making this a reality.

> *Reflective Portfolio Activity*
> Name five things you consider to be part of your own ethnicity or culture. Prepare a poster that shows how these five things make you unique. Explain how these five things can contribute to your setting.

Diversity

Every child in your setting is unique with a unique set of gifts that they bring to the setting. Some children have personalities that can light up a room, others may be quiet and unassuming by nature, while others may have disabilities or abilities that make them individual. No two children are exactly alike (not even identical twins) and the uniqueness of the child brings something to the setting and makes it stand out by their contribution to everyday activities.

Diversity is about difference. As a supervisor you need to have a rounded approach to the needs of the children in your setting and ensure that you and your staff provide a setting that is responsive to the differences that exist (remember, some of these differences may only be noticed after the child has joined your setting). As supervisor, you should look at all aspects of the difference and put systems in place that facilitate all aspects of that difference, which can be numerous.

Opposite are some examples of issues that may arise in an environment that embraces diversity. As a supervisor, you need to ensure that:
- You are aware of each child's individuality, which is often achieved through a carefully worded and detailed application form.
- Conversations with the child, parents/guardians and key workers that might alert you to each child's diverse needs are noted and acted on.

- Observations carried out in the setting (e.g. concept attainment may alert you to a gifted child who needs more stimulation) are discussed in a systematic way with the team who work with each child.
- You take note of medical records or multi-professional interactions that may alert you to differences in relation to individual children who need facilitation in the setting.
- Reviews of each child in the setting are put in place so that nothing is missed in relation to that child.

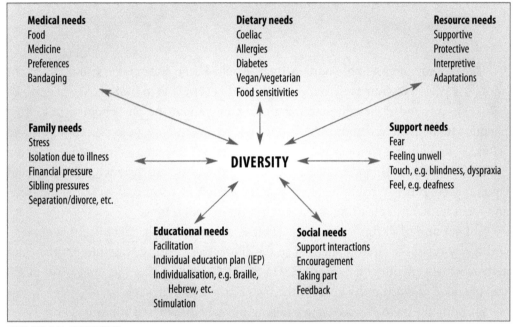

FIGURE 6.3: DIVERSITY

With current changes in pre-school services to include all abilities in the one setting, diversity will become an important part of any supervisor's work. Being aware of a child's right to achieve to the best of their potential, as outlined in the UNCRC, must be an important part of the approach you take to diversity in your setting.

Reflective Portfolio Activity
Observe four children in your setting with diverse needs and explain what the needs of each child are and how they differ from each other. For each child, explain how the setting provides support to ensure their needs are being met in terms of their diversity.

SEVEN

Child-centred Approaches

Without pre-school children there would be no pre-school setting and your vision of your preferred setting would never come to fruition. We have taken a rounded view in describing everything about the pre-school setting, from planning to the preferred approach of your ideal setting through your reflective portfolio activities. In outlining your job as a supervisor in an ECCE setting, considerable skills are needed to interact with government, education, health, welfare, parental, and social and emotional concepts. What is involved is a negotiation of resources, staff, training, time and focus in order to create an efficiently run pre-school setting.

At the centre of all this is the child. There is no point in engaging in all that effort if, at the very basis, the child is ancillary to the effort. You are duty bound to put the child at the centre of anything that takes place in the ECCE setting. The very concept of ECCE was intended to reach many goals in the lives of the children, such as:

- Ensuring the child has access to enabling pre-school care and education.
- Providing support for children at risk.
- Integrating pre-school childcare with an approach to education.
- Providing children with a good foundation for later life by setting the groundwork at the pre-school stage.
- Providing for suitably trained professional staff who are responsive to children's needs.
- Reversing disadvantage, however it is experienced, in a child's life with a sense of belonging and achievement.
- Providing an opportunity for each child to reach their best potential.
- Creating childcare settings where children are challenged and stimulated.
- Creating a palpable sense of self-worth for each child.
- Ensuring the intervention of a professional approach to the lives of pre-school children.

When we looked earlier at the dynamics of the supervisor's role, we saw how diverse the approach to childcare and education is. In every aspect of your work with children you must plan to meet the needs of each individual child and balance the necessary strategies for doing so with the ongoing work of your staff.

Planning

Planning for the care of each individual child requires a concerted, consistent and clear system. In Chapter 6 we looked at how information is received on the needs of each child, but all the information-gathering in the world will make no difference to the child unless you put a system in place that caters for their needs.

Any planning process should employ a number of steps, each informing the next stage in the process.

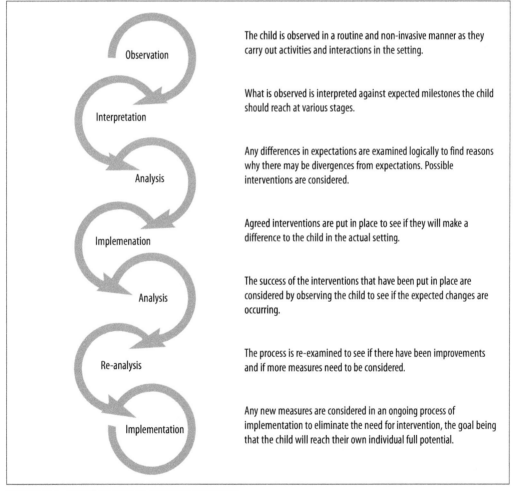

Observation	The child is observed in a routine and non-invasive manner as they carry out activities and interactions in the setting.
Interpretation	What is observed is interpreted against expected milestones the child should reach at various stages.
Analysis	Any differences in expectations are examined logically to find reasons why there may be divergences from expectations. Possible interventions are considered.
Implemenation	Agreed interventions are put in place to see if they will make a difference to the child in the actual setting.
Analysis	The success of the interventions that have been put in place are considered by observing the child to see if the expected changes are occurring.
Re-analysis	The process is re-examined to see if there have been improvements and if more measures need to be considered.
Implementation	Any new measures are considered in an ongoing process of implementation to eliminate the need for intervention, the goal being that the child will reach their own individual full potential.

FIGURE 7.1: STEPS IN THE PLANNING PROCESS

This is not a once-off process but an explanation of the way in which each child's needs should be incorporated into your work in an integrated way. For a child with more needs, this can be a protracted process, but it will always have that child's needs as its base. Not every change or intervention that is needed relates to the child: changes may in fact mean looking at the resources or procedures in the setting (for example, when it is decided that a child needs a nap on a particular day for some reason). Making sure that your staff are alert, informed, re-active and experienced in finding solutions that will facilitate children's needs is paramount; and you are responsible for facilitating, listening to and enabling your staff. In turn, this creates an environment that allows a child to find solutions for themselves in the future by following the processes of trial and elimination that are evident in the above process.

Plans for each child will be broken into:

- Long-term plan (from baby to schoolchild).
- Medium-term plan (from wobbler to toddler).
- Short-term plan (from morning to evening).
- Detailed activity plan (getting a child ready to go outside and play).

All plans feed into each other and must be integrated with the child at the centre of the process so that the child is both considered and consulted.

Planning also feeds into curriculum planning for children. It is important to plan to meet curriculum goals in the process of evaluating children's progress, as the very essence of a pre-school setting is to prepare children for school. In school, children will be faced with bigger challenges and will benefit if any support needs have been identified before they get to school, as this makes for an easy progression and immediate settling in, which leads to better attainment.

Reflective Portfolio Activity
You have been asked to draw up a plan for one child in your setting who is learning to write.
Explain how you would go about this and what you would include in each of the short-term, medium-term and long-term plans. How would you change these plans if the child had a specific disability affecting their fine motor skills?

Holistic Approaches

The smallest of children have their own individual ways of letting you know when they want something – even a small baby will quickly learn to cry to get attention when they need it. This ability is one that every childcare worker is trained to recognise and all your staff should be well versed in the ways in which the children in your setting demonstrate their own individual preferences. Not every child, however, is capable of sound, in which case observing facial expressions or body language will alert you to their needs. Once again, the information you have about a child will assist you in knowing how a child prefers to express their needs or anxieties. The child themselves may not be aware of how their body gives clues to their needs (e.g. for some children it may be uncontrolled fiddling when anxious) and in such situations observing the child may be the first clue to knowing what is going on. This is particularly important when a child is unable to express their needs orally, either because they have not attained the language to do so or because they do not know the word for what they feel.

A holistic approach is about knowing that the child requires a rounded approach to their needs. They want to experience as much as they can in your setting, but this involves opening up opportunities for children to engage, explore, experience, enjoy, expand and seek opportunities to learn and flourish in your setting and in the wider community. Your role as supervisor is to encourage flexibility to allow all this to happen for each child, and you should also be aware of what the child needs outside your setting that will add to their ability to get the most out of the experience.

Some children may display special talents, which should be encouraged. Parents may not be aware of your observations and in these cases you are advocating for the child when you set changes in motion that will develop the child's skills. Where children have been assessed as needing extra assistance, such as occupational therapy, psychology or other professional interventions, you are similarly advocating on behalf of the child when you encourage the professional involved to come to the setting to discuss how the setting can assist the child's progress. In such cases, the interactions between professionals will benefit the child as the message from each is supported and reinforced by the others.

Preparing children for their later life experiences is an important part of the ECCE experience that involves social, emotional, welfare and wellness areas. Encouraging children to advocate for each other, to be responsible for their own actions, to acknowledge the rights of the other children in the setting and to contribute to the way in which the setting interacts with them by stating their preferences is encouraging a holistic approach for the child. The child has a say and contributes by learning to understand the interaction of rights and responsibilities as well as the connection between actions and consequences. This, together with respect, will ensure that the ECCE system is contributing to the development of moral, honest and responsible citizens of the future. As supervisor, you should consider ways in which you can involve children in the operation of the setting. Giving them responsibilities appropriate to their age and stage of development, such as including children in decision-making about the choices they have, will encourage them to express themselves and be ready for each stage of their own holistic development.

Behaviour Management

Children often model the behaviour they see around them, and in a setting that has a positive approach there is a sense of commitment, understanding, being positive about experiences and being included in decision-making and their own development, as we have already outlined. There should be a written policy on behaviour management in every setting so that all the stakeholders know and accept the consequences of behaviour that is not conducive to a good working relationship. While it is easy to say that we should accentuate positive behaviour and challenge negative behaviour, it is more important to understand why an individual child's behaviour is challenging at any particular moment.

Children themselves understand that when everybody is behaving, things are more productive, positive, calm and happy, but there are some times when children may not even realise that their behaviour is affecting others. Sometimes children need support to improve their behaviour in these situations, which can arise for any number of reasons, including:

- Feelings of exclusion.
- Need for attention.
- Being left waiting unnecessarily.
- Feeling unwell.
- Attention deficit spectrum.
- Autism.
- Stress at home.
- The arrival of a new sibling who commands attention.
- New children in the setting.
- Change of room in the setting.
- Sensory deficit issues.
- Change of circumstances.
- Lack of sleep.
- Hunger.
- Feeling of being treated unfairly.
- Inability to verbalise feelings.
- Change of routine.
- Boredom and lack of challenge.

In every setting, the issues of behaviour that materialise are as individual as the children themselves, but the key to tackling behaviour management issues is to be fully informed about the circumstances of the behaviour. Giving a child stickers to show they have reached goals will not necessarily motivate them to behave better if the root cause of the boredom which led to the behaviour is not also tackled. When a child has passed the stage where stickers impress them, it is time to move to another tactic and this will only be achieved by working with the child and supporting both the child and their key worker in bringing about change. If a holistic approach has been taken in the setting, the information and supports will be available in the setting to facilitate consistent behaviour management.

As a supervisor, it is important that you support all the children in the setting and ensure that safe, fair and consistent approaches are taken to behaviour management. Listening, talking, respecting, watching, supporting, consistency and explaining form the basis of good behaviour management policies. Responding to children's needs in the setting is fundamental to any approach that is taken to make sure that behaviour is not challenging and limiting for the child. Training for all staff should be consistent with the rights of each child, the setting and the goal of a happy and enabling environment for each child. Realising that behaviour management is an individual concept in relation to each child is important and you as supervisor are required to consider reactions and interventions on an individual basis.

> ### Reflective Portfolio Activity
> Obtain a copy of your setting's behaviour management policy and explain how three specific behaviour management issues are dealt with in the setting. Reflect on how well you feel the policy meets the needs of the children, staff and parents in the setting. Would you change anything, and if so, why?

The Importance of Fun in a Child's Life

Many childcare manuals say little about the importance of fun in a child's life, but it is a very important element that should not be overlooked. Ensuring that there is time for fun in the setting is often overlooked in preference to having things run smoothly. Anybody who has ever seen a child jump in a puddle must have seen the sheer pleasure a child gets from the fun of creating a splash. Laughter produced by fun is such an important thing in every child's life that there should be a slot in your timetable every day for some fun.

Fun breaks down boundaries between children, allows them to challenge boundaries in a risk-assessed way and supports learning when incorporated positively in the setting.

The simple fun of blowing bubbles allows children to enjoy aerobic exercise without realising it and the joy of chasing bubbles can involve a child who is finding it hard to fit into a new setting and provide exercise in the process. Making up silly words can elicit great laugher from children while extending their creative skills, as can writing funny stories about anything the child can imagine. The development of the child's imagination is supported by thinking up the most outrageous scenario, as is their vocabulary in the description process.

As a supervisor, you will be required to be resourceful in creating opportunities for learning, and incorporating fun opens up a whole range of possibilities.

Reflective Portfolio Activity

Having observed how play has been incorporated in child development in your setting, explain in your own words how children benefit from a balance of play, learning and care and the place of fun in this process in relation to one specific child (remember, you should not identify the child in your reflective diary so as to protect the child's privacy).

EIGHT

The Importance of Play in the ECCE Setting

P lay in the life of a child in an ECCE setting is multifaceted and involves concepts that are at the very heart of childcare and the education of the pre-school child, as can be seen in Figure 8.1.

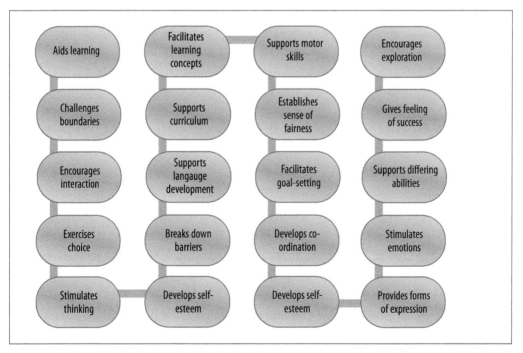

FIGURE 8.1: PLAY IN THE ECCE SETTING

The range of materials and opportunities for play are important in any ECCE setting and both Síolta and Aistear provide prompts as to how the setting can be made play-friendly and how toys, materials, imagination and settings can support children in the pre-school setting. Play meets the PILES of child development: the physical (fine and gross motor skills are developed), intellectual (children learn how things work and are related), language (children learn to talk to each other as they play), emotional (they learn about feelings and their own emotions in the process) and social (co-operating, sharing and helping each other) aspects, as we can see in all the above elements of play.

However, play is not just about putting everything in front of a child and letting them get on with it. It includes storage, display, access and choice, which must be facilitated by all in the setting. Suitable materials must take into account the individual needs of each child, which may include the need to vary or adapt toys so that children with different needs and abilities get as much from the toy as any other child. Every child should be given the possibility of choosing what they want to play with and how.

Child-led Play

Anybody who has ever seen a child play with an empty box at Christmas, when there are many toys around, will understand the concept of child-led play. Watching a small baby touch and hit something that hangs in their cot is the start of child-led play. The child initiates the adventure and creates their own reality from the play they engage in. Adults may supervise the activity to ensure it is safe, but the child decides where the activity goes after that.

Looking at the elements of play above, it is important that the child is allowed to engage in such play opportunities, as it encourages independence and a sense of freedom and adventure. People often make the mistake of getting involved and directing the way in which small children play, but real child-led play follows no agenda except that set by the child.

Access needs to be provided to the toys, dress-up clothes and other resources that facilitate child-led play and they must be at a level the child can reach or access themselves so that they can initiate the play. As a supervisor, you need to store resources so that children have the choice to initiate their own activities and to make sure that staff in your setting facilitate the opportunities that arise. This may mean that routines and detailed daily plans should be flexible enough to allow divergence that is child led.

Sometimes play is a safe place for a child who wishes to forget about stresses they have, an illness that may be their constant companion, or silence that they crave. As a supervisor, you must be aware that the child may have a need to opt out for a while and you must allow this in the setting. It allows the child to order things in their mind, block out what they don't want to deal with at that time and put their thoughts in order. It may even be a way in which they express their fears. All of this should be supported rather than led so the child gets what they need from the situation they create for themselves. Noting a child's need for such play is an important job for the key worker and the rest of your team, which you as supervisor support in your procedures and practices.

Child-centred Play

As we have seen, play forms a significant part in the development of a child, and for this reason there should be a focus on times when play is planned. Child-centred play often involves looking at ways in which play can be encouraged for the child, with (but not always) a purpose such as learning how to do things for themselves. In addition, child-centred play asks the child what types of toys or resources they wish to play with. *Ready Steady Play! A National Play Policy* was published by the Office of the Minister for Children in 2004 to address the importance of play in children's lives and provides an overview of the importance of allowing children to have a say in their play options. Putting a system in place for your setting that addresses the issues raised in *Ready Steady Play!* will ensure that your setting is meeting best practice.

Children who have different abilities, disabilities or special needs will all get something different from play, provided it is child centred: any adjustments to provide access or usability must support the child's specific needs. Children who are in hospital settings, for instance, may look for reassurance from the play they engage in and may create scenarios where they discuss what is happening to them. Online contact with their friends, such as Solas, provides opportunities for sick children to play online games with their peers from school or home settings and helps dispel a sense of isolation, which may occur with very sick children.

As a supervisor, you might deal with a child who is absent from your setting for long periods due to illness, so you should try to provide a sense of continuity for that child by facilitating interactions when they are able, in a way that is centred on that child's needs at that time. Keeping yourself and your staff informed of such interventions is very much a part of your job as supervisor and the reward is the full integration of every child into your setting in a way that meets their needs.

Adult-led Play

When you as an adult provide opportunities to engage children in play and at the same time instruct the child in how they should engage with that play, you are providing adult-led play opportunities. The child does not necessarily know where the play is leading and this can often create situations where there is no independence of thought in relation to the play being undertaken. This can create situations where the child is fully dependent on the adult for the next step and there are frequent pauses to check that the child is following the instructions being given. The play is more about instruction from the adult than play led by the child or even the child's imagination.

Sometimes children need adult-led play as it may be the only way in which they can engage in play in a meaningful way. This may arise in severe disability or even in very small children who have not learned to initiate play or are reluctant to do so for some reason. Children recovering from abuse may need the adult to lead the play until they trust the situation they find themselves in. Where this is part of a recovery process, it should be facilitated with support from other professionals with suitable training.

Adult-supervised play is preferable to adult-led play as there is an overseeing role for the adult rather than a directing role. Often the instruction process makes a huge difference to choice in the child's play and this is more enabling for the child's development processes. For a small child, there may be elements of teaching a child to follow rules in adult-led play, and while this does have a part to play in a child's development, it should be tempered with supervision and a say in how things progress in a truly enabling ECCE setting. Thus, a supervisor should oversee a mixture of adult-led play where necessary but should enable it to move to adult-supervised play so that the child gets enjoyment and fun from the play.

Indoor and Outdoor Play

Every child in an ECCE setting should have access to indoor and outdoor play to have variety, to get fresh air during their day and to ensure that they are healthy. There is no formula or specific ratio of the balance between indoor and outdoor play and there should be opportunities for both in your setting. Ensuring that some of the play equipment in your setting can be used both indoors and outdoors allows for flexibility in creating a mix of indoor and outdoor play: equipment can be used outdoors and brought in if there is a change in the weather.

There is much talk about Norwegian pre-school opportunities for children to learn outdoors and Forest Schools have attracted much comment. There is definitely more space to run around and stretch when children are outdoors and this can be very enabling for some children, but others prefer not to get cold or wet and indeed some parents may voice their preferences. In Ireland, we have not engaged in a predominance of either indoor or outdoor play, though there might be a little bias towards indoor play to compensate for our climate. Every setting should provide their own rationale for the choices they make. As supervisor, you should be well versed in the benefits of each in the setting and should ensure that the balance is for the benefit of the children and not necessarily for the comfort of the staff or others. Extra clothing in winter or sun protection in the summer may be required so that children are adequately protected from weather extremes. Having flexible plans means that every opportunity is maximised. Snowmen don't make themselves!

Risk Assessment

Risk assessment is about weighing an action against a possible reaction (negative or positive) and making a decision based on that assessment. An adult often does this automatically on a daily basis. Children also need to learn to make mistakes and learn from them or make choices that may or may not prove rewarding in order for the skill of risk assessment to be grasped. Balancing on something can be exhilarating for a child because there is sense of danger, but danger should be tempered with a sense of achievement and this happens if the child learns what is needed to keep themselves safe while enjoying the risk. Learning boundaries is very much a part of every child's life and overprotection can be a form of cruelty. Learning that actions have consequences is also important for a child's welfare development that should be supported in the ECCE setting.

As a supervisor, you need to carry out risk assessments with your staff in relation to health and safety in your setting, but talking processes through with a child will also inform them of potential risks they face and how to avoid them. A balance must be struck in your setting against not allowing children to try new experiences and the possibility of hurting themselves in the process. Some children, such as those with dyspraxia, may have an over- or under-sensitivity to touch or pain, and in this case the risk assessment outcome will be different depending on the child's sensory reactions. Being informed about all the children in your setting is important in such situations and risk assessment should therefore be a constant process in the setting to meet the best interests of each child. Parents must understand the processes involved in risk assessment and how important it is in the child's development. This can then support the element of challenge in a child's life in the setting.

Creating Challenges for Children

Children are developing and learning in your setting every minute they are there, and creating challenges provides the developing child with a sense of achievement when they manage something they were unable to do just a short time before. A child who has learned how to put their coat on independently will be even more satisfied if they also learn to zip it up. However, they should also acknowledge each part of the process so that they feel they have achieved something and their self-esteem is not dampened by the existence of the next step. Challenge provides interest, and for gifted children who are not challenged in the setting, lack of challenge may create behaviour issues when boredom sets in, just as behaviour issues may arise if the challenge is beyond the child, as they might feel inadequate and demotivated. However, children are not performing monkeys and challenge should not just be a matter of learning a trick.

Learning is achieved through challenge and, when properly managed, healthy challenge supports a sense of purpose and wonder for a child. You and your staff should create environments and resources that allow a child to reach goals and learn to challenge themselves so they can take ownership of their own learning. This is a gradual process and will involve planning to set up the challenges that will motivate the individual child depending on their needs. Knowing when a child is ready for a challenge is a skill, but one which you and your staff should be proficient at if you have enough information to know what will challenge the individual child.

Reflective Portfolio Activity

In your setting, identify the following types of play:

▶ Adult led
▶ Child led
▶ Adult supervised
▶ Play that can take place either indoors or outdoors

In relation to one particular child, explain when you use each method for that specific child and what challenges this presents for you and the child.

NINE

Curriculum Design and Planning

Aistear is a good companion to any curriculum process in a pre-school setting and every member of your team must understand the place of curriculum in what you do in your setting. We discussed different approaches to childcare in Chapter 6 and the approach chosen for your setting may influence how you incorporate curriculum into your setting, how you assist children to reach goals and how you, your staff and the children form those goals in the first place.

Under Article 5 of the Child Care (Pre-School Services) (No. 2) (Amendment) Regulations 2006, every childcare worker is required to 'ensure that each child's learning, development and well-being is facilitated within the daily life of the service through the provision of the appropriate opportunities, experiences, activities, interaction, materials and equipment, having regard to the age and stage of development of the child and the child's cultural context'. In other words, they are required to have a curriculum for each child that is unique to that child and that child's stage, age, development, abilities and background.

Approaches to Planning

Curriculum in a pre-school setting is a process of designing a learning path for a pre-school child based on a process of observation and established goals and milestones that are expected to be met by each individual child. Curriculum may be set as a minimum that is expected to be achieved in terms of learning and experiences for each child, as outlined in Aistear. Every child is different and the pace and method with which they learn also differs, which is why any curriculum plan should be individually tailored and be unique to the particular child in question. Knowing and understanding what is needed in your setting requires you to be well informed about the potential of each child and what supports need to be put in place so that the child can avail of the opportunities that will ensure they reach their best potential. The concept of potential is not a minimum but an unlimited possibility, and this requires you, as supervisor, to expand the possibilities for every child in your care.

If you look back at the wording in the Child Care (Pre-School) (No. 2) (Amendment) Regulations 2006 above, it is important to note the words used and the interpretation that is required in how you as a supervisor approach the concept of curriculum in your setting.

Daily life of the service

Curriculum should be seamless within the setting, which indicates an expectation that the concept of curriculum should be a part of everything you do and should be a method of doing things that fits into the seamless interpretation of curriculum. Asking a child how you can help them achieve what they want to do is a way of teaching them where to go for assistance and also a way of actually offering assistance. This should be borne in mind in relation to the messages you and your team give children, whether you intend them or not. Role modelling is an important part of the job of any childcare and education worker.

Facilitated

There is an expectation that things that are done will wrap around the concept of curriculum rather than the other way around. The child's development needs should therefore be interwoven into how things are approached in the setting. For example, a child who wants to learn how to work out a rhythm may be taught how to do it using everyday objects such as pencils in a pot or rice in a bottle if those are the sounds the child wants to create at that time.

Opportunities

There should be a recognition that everyday activities can be expanded upon to make opportunities for the child to broaden their learning, development and well-being. Saying good morning and shaking hands with the child every day, for instance, is a way of providing opportunities for the child to develop their social skills. You should always be on the look-out for ways in which to incorporate the development of the child's skills in the things you and your staff do.

Experiences

There should be ample experiences built into the pre-school setting every day to allow a child to develop within the curriculum you create for them. This should be a flexible concept and the rate at which the child achieves development goals should be openly tested to ensure that they are challenged at their own pace. As supervisor, you should check that your team is constantly reviewing the achievements of each child to ensure that they are reaching their best potential, even if that means you need to offer more support or seek additional expertise to ensure that they do so. A child who has a specific learning difficulty should be able to rely on you to find the necessary supports needed when you become aware that such a need exists. For instance, discovering that one of the children in your care has developmental co-ordination delay should prompt you to learn about the implications of this for the child and to find out how you can support the child's learning and development with your resources and in your setting.

Activities

At all times, activities should be encouraged that allow a child to learn in innovative ways in your setting and timetables and indeed within your planning cycles. Playing outside in the snow, for instance, could be an opportunity to introduce the scientific concept of frozen water and also to see and measure volumes of water in a different context than just on paper in a book. Opportunities are endless with the proper use and application of imagination and foresight on your part.

Materials

The use of materials in your setting should be flexible and open to interpretation by children and staff in the pursuit of challenge and learning. An example of this would be allowing a child to fax a picture to their parent at work: this shows them how to use a piece of technology you already have and how to keep in touch with people using their ingenuity. There are endless opportunities, and if you are open to the use of materials, this is a good way of allowing the child to explore possibilities too.

Equipment

Equipment should be regularly checked to make sure it is suitable for purpose, as required by the HSE, but equipment should also be flexible enough to allow each child to reach their potential at any specific development stage. For instance, books should be regularly changed so that they provide adequate stimulation for the children who are at the reading stage. Where a child has a particular interest, the books available to them in the setting should encourage their reading development as well as their personal interest.

Visiting a local library could assist in the process: this serves to show the child how to get more material, how to borrow books and how to discuss their requirements with others. Computers and e-books may also serve this purpose. As supervisor, you should be open to the possibilities of using all equipment in the curriculum context.

At all stages, you and your team should be able to work out ways of facilitating and encouraging adventure and challenge for every child. You should consult with the child so that they have a role in the curriculum adventure rather than being a bystander in the whole process. You do have a responsibility to keep records of the ways in which you carry out curriculum in relation to each child and some of the organisations to which you subscribe will have booklets to guide you.

Remember, however, that to simply copy another person's way of doing things can make you somewhat limited in the way you use your imagination in the setting. Your recording process should obviously correspond with the HSE inspection tool so that minimum standards are met, but it should also be individual to your setting and the specific child to whom it relates. Every child deserves that you and your team engage in the curriculum so that you are aware of their achievements, challenges, their needs in the process and how best to help them reach the challenges you provide with a sense of well-being that encourages further development.

Curriculum Design

We have already seen that the process of curriculum should be individual to each child and that each child should be facilitated to achieve the goals set out for them in the curriculum. This is especially important for children with different support needs, as you need to plan to provide the supports required in a timely manner at the most opportune time for that child. This is about the preparedness of you and your team, and the resources you employ. Some children may need to review and learn in different ways, which can be worked out in consultation with the child's parents or guardians. A trip to the Natural History Museum, for instance, is a good way of reviewing the concept of how big a mammoth was for a child learning about mammoths as part of a curriculum plan.

Flexibility is a significant part of any curriculum plan for an individual child and there should be no sense of 'one size fits all' in any curriculum planning in your setting. The interests of the child may form the most important part of that child's curriculum design: if concepts are introduced in a way that matches the child's interests, they are more likely to be receptive to the new ideas. It is also important to understand what is going on in the child's life when you introduce something new, and this can be best learned from conversations with children and their parents or guardians. This will also help inform cultural, ability or access aspects that might affect how a curriculum plan is developed for that child. For example, it would not be appropriate to suggest that a child will understand what colour a lemon is by showing them one if that child is blind.

Encouraging children to enjoy their development journey is a huge part of successful curriculum planning and ensures that even small steps are seen as being part of a bigger process as well as a successful accomplishment which leads to other possibilities. Aistear is described as a curriculum framework and every pre-school setting will be required to provide curriculum around its themes of:

- Well-being.
- Identity and belonging.
- Communicating.
- Exploring and thinking.

In its outline, Aistear describes ways in which each theme can be achieved and gives suggestions as to how this might be planned for in your setting. As already stated, this should be the minimum done, as to limit any child is to fail to meet their right to grow and develop to their best potential.

In outlining the concept of well-being, Aistear sets out aims and learning goals that must be followed and indeed recorded so that each child has a journal of the steps they have undergone in their individual learning and development journey. This should be an individual portfolio for each child that will go with them when they move on from your setting. This ensures that every child has a plan that is being followed. Importantly, it is not the exact same plan for each child, as needs and progress will differ depending on the child themselves.

The aims and learning goals for well-being as set out in Aistear are as follows.

TABLE 9.1: AISTEAR AIMS AND LEARNING GOALS FOR WELL-BEING

Aims	Learning goals
Aim 1 Children will be strong psychologically and socially.	In partnership with the adult, children will: 1. Make strong attachments and develop warm and supportive relationships with family, peers and adults in out-of-home settings and in their community. 2. Be aware of and name their own feelings and understand that others may have different feelings. 3. Handle transitions and changes well. 4. Be confident and self-reliant. 5. Respect themselves, others and the environment. 6. Make decisions and choices about their own learning and development.

continued next page ⟶

Aims	Learning goals
Aim 2 Children will be as healthy and fit as they can be.	In partnership with the adult, children will: 1. Gain increasing control and co-ordination of body movements. 2. Be aware of their bodies, their bodily functions and their changing abilities. 3. Discover, explore and refine gross and fine motor skills. 4. Use self-help skills in caring for their own bodies. 5. Show good judgment when taking risks. 6. Make healthy choices and demonstrate positive attitudes to nutrition, hygiene, exercise and routine.
Aim 3 Children will be creative and spiritual.	In partnership with the adult, children will: 1. Express themselves creatively and experience the arts. 2. Express themselves through a variety of types of play. 3. Develop and nurture their sense of wonder and awe. 4. Become reflective and think flexibly. 5. Care for the environment. 6. Understand that others may have beliefs and values different to their own.
Aim 4 Children will have positive outlooks on learning and on life.	In partnership with the adult, children will: 1. Show increasing independence and be able to make choices and decisions. 2. Demonstrate a sense of mastery and belief in their own abilities and display learning dispositions such as determination and perseverance. 3. Think positively, take learning risks and become resilient and resourceful when things go wrong. 4. Motivate themselves and welcome and seek challenge. 5. Respect life, their own and others', and know that life has a meaning and purpose. 6. Be active citizens.

Source: Aistear: The Early Childhood Curriculum Framework.

Obviously, the way you and your staff approach each learning goal will depend on the age, ability and level of understanding of each individual child and your key staff will be the people who will keep you informed about the development of each child in relation to the learning goals. However, as a supervisor you also have an overseeing role in this process and you need to keep yourself informed on how staff members are approaching the required goals. Because each child is an individual, innovations in the way curriculum is taught or guided may be introduced by each staff member. (Aistear offers suggested scenarios in relation to the learning goals, but these are indicative and interpretation is encouraged as long as the goals are reached, recorded, reviewed and have the desired learning and development outcomes for the individual children.)

The corresponding Aistear aims and learning goals for identity and belonging are as follows.

TABLE 9.2: AISTEAR AIMS AND LEARNING GOALS FOR IDENTITY AND BELONGING

Aims	Learning goals
Aim 1 Children will have strong self-identities and will feel respected and affirmed as unique individuals with their own life stories.	In partnership with the adult, the child will: 1. Build respectful relationships with others. 2. Appreciate the features that make a person special and unique (name, size, hair, hand and footprint, gender, birthday). 3. Understand that as individuals they are separate from others with their own needs, interests and abilities. 4. Have a sense of 'who they are' and be able to describe their backgrounds, strengths and abilities. 5. Feel valued and see themselves and their interests reflected in the environment. 6. Express their own ideas, preferences and needs and have these responded to with respect and consistency.
Aim 2 Children will have a sense of group identity where links with their family and community are acknowledged and extended.	In partnership with the adult, the child will: 1. Feel that they have a place and a right to belong to the group. 2. Know that members of their family and community are positively acknowledged and welcomed. 3. Be able to share personal experiences about their own families and cultures and come to know that there is a diversity of family structures, cultures and backgrounds. 4. Understand and take part in routines, customs, festivals and celebrations. 5. See themselves as part of a wider community and know about their local area, including some of its places, features and people. 6. Understand the different roles of people in the community.
Aim 3 Children will be able to express their rights and show understanding and regard for the identity, rights and views of others.	In partnership with the adult, children will: 1. Express their views and help make decisions in matters that affect them. 2. Understand the rules and the boundaries of acceptable behaviour. 3. Interact, work co-operatively and help others. 4. Be aware of and respect others' needs, rights, feelings, culture, language, background and religious beliefs. 5. Have a sense of social justice and recognise and deal with unfair behaviour. 6. Demonstrate the skills of co-operation, responsibility, negotiation and conflict resolution.
Aim 4 Children will see themselves as capable learners.	In partnership with the adult, children will: 1. Develop a broad range of abilities and interests. 2. Show an awareness of their own unique strengths, abilities and learning styles and be willing to share their skills and knowledge with others. 3. Show increasing confidence and self-assurance in directing their own learning. 4. Demonstrate dispositions like curiosity, persistence and responsibility. 5. Experience learning opportunities that are based on personal interests and linked to their home, community and culture. 6. Be motivated and begin to think about and recognise their own progress and achievements.

Source: Aistear: The Early Childhood Curriculum Framework.

Clearly, from the wording and the learning outcome expectations, you need to have ongoing consultation with and feedback from the children involved in the curriculum you are implementing. It is important to note that Aistear sets out to ensure that the child achieves the stated learning outcomes 'in partnership with the adult', so there is a presumed supporting role that your staff are required to be part of. Once again, the age and stage of the child has to be taken into account and this should be an ongoing part of the records maintained on any individual child in the setting by you and your staff. Pacing the work that is being achieved by each child may be affected by the ethos or mission statement of the setting, but it should be in the child's best interests and follow their own wishes or stated preferences, depending on their age and stage of development.

Providing resourceful and effective ways in which to incorporate child development goals into curriculum will take consultation, imagination, constant review and challenge so that all people in the child's life are working with the child themselves to incorporate the rights that the child will now be familiar with in a way which allows the child to take ownership of their own behaviour, rights and responsibilities.

Aistear's aims and learning goals for communicating are as follows.

TABLE 9.3: AISTEAR AIMS AND LEARNING GOALS FOR COMMUNICATION

Aims	Learning goals
Aim 1 Children will use non-verbal communication skills.	In partnership with the adult, children will: 1. Use a range of body movements, facial expressions and early vocalisations to show feelings and share information. 2. Understand and use non-verbal communication rules, such as turn-taking and making eye contact. 3. Interpret and respond to non-verbal communication by others. 4. Understand and respect that some people will rely on non-verbal communication as their main way of interacting with others. 5. Combine non-verbal and verbal communication to get their point across. 6. Express themselves creatively and imaginatively using non-verbal communication.
Aim 2 Children will use language.	In partnership with the adult, children will: 1. Interact with other children and adults by listening, discussing and taking turns in conversation. 2. Explore sound, pattern, rhythm and repetition in language. 3. Use an expanding vocabulary of words and phrases and show a growing understanding of syntax and meaning. 4. Use language with confidence and competence for giving and receiving information, asking questions, requesting, refusing, negotiating, problem-solving, imagining and recreating roles and situations and clarifying thinking, ideas and feelings. 5. Become proficient users of at least one language and have an awareness and appreciation of other languages. 6. Be positive about their home language and know that they can use different languages to communicate with different people and in different situations.
Aim 3 Children will broaden their understanding of the world by making sense of experiences through language.	In partnership with the adult, the child will: 1. Use language to interpret experiences, to solve problems and to clarify thinking, ideas and feelings. 2. Use books and ICT for fun, to gain information and broaden their understanding of the world. 3. Build an awareness of the variety of symbols (pictures, print, numbers) used to communicate and understand that these can be read by others. 4. Become familiar with and use a variety of print in an enjoyable and meaningful way. 5. Have opportunities to use a variety of mark-making materials and implements in an enjoyable and meaningful way. 6. Develop counting skills and a growing understanding of the meaning and use of numbers and mathematical language in an enjoyable and meaningful way.
Aim 4 Children will express themselves creatively and imaginatively.	In partnership with the adult, children will: 1. Share their feelings, thoughts and ideas by storytelling, making art, moving to music, role-playing, problem-solving and responding to these experiences. 2. Express themselves through the visual arts using skills such as cutting, drawing, gluing, sticking, painting, building, printing, sculpting and sewing. 3. Listen to and respond to a variety of types of music, sing songs and make music using instruments. 4. Use language to imagine and recreate roles and experiences. 5. Respond to and create literacy experiences through story, poetry, song and drama. 6. Show confidence in trying new things, taking risks and thinking creatively.

Source: Aistear: The Early Childhood Curriculum Framework.

Communicating is a goal that lends itself to the use of technology, which can enhance children's communication skills, for example in language acquisition and the ability to make themselves understood. Allowing a child to send a picture by fax, email or mobile phone is a way of incorporating curriculum into the environment the child lives in and encourages development in all areas of a child's life. Keeping up to date with communication possibilities may be a challenge, particularly in relation to ensuring that privacy issues are adequately dealt with. Using new technology as suggested may also allow a child whose mother tongue is not English, and who may be reluctant or unable to communicate in English, to take part in communication activities, as they may be more willing to communicate with somebody outside the setting until they have mastered the language.

The final theme for Aistear is exploring and thinking.

TABLE 9.4: AISTEAR AIMS AND LEARNING GOALS FOR EXPLORING AND THINKING

Aims	Learning goals
Aim 1 Children will learn about and make sense of the world around them.	In partnership with the adult, children will: 1. Engage, explore and experiment in their environment and use new physical skills, including skills to manipulate objects and materials. 2. Demonstrate a growing understanding of themselves and others in their community. 3. Develop an understanding of change as part of their lives. 4. Learn about the natural environment and its features, materials, animals and plants and their own responsibility as carers. 5. Develop a sense of time, shape, space and place. 6. Come to understand concepts such as matching, comparing, ordering, sorting, size, weight, height, length, capacity and money in an enjoyable and meaningful way.
Aim 2 Children will develop and use skills and strategies for observing, questioning, investigating, understanding, negotiating and problem-solving and come to see themselves as explorers and thinkers.	In partnership with the adult, children will: 1. Recognise patterns and make connections and associations between new learning and what they already know. 2. Gather and use information from different sources using their increasing cognitive, physical and social skills. 3. Use their experience and information to explore and develop working theories about how the world works, and think about how and why they learn things. 4. Demonstrate their ability to reason, negotiate and think logically. 5. Collaborate with others to share interests and to solve problems confidently. 6. Use their creativity and imagination to think of new ways to solve problems.
Aim 3 Children will explore ways to represent ideas, feelings, thoughts, objects and actions through symbols.	In partnership with the adult, children will: 1. Make marks and use drawing, painting and model-making to record objects, events and ideas. 2. Become familiar with and associate symbols (pictures, numbers, letters and words) with the things they represent. 3. Build awareness of the variety of symbols (pictures, print, numbers) used to communicate and use these in an enjoyable and meaningful way, leading to early reading and writing. 4. Express feelings, thoughts and ideas through improvising, moving, playing, talking, writing, storytelling, music and art. 5. Use letters, words, sentences, numbers, signs, pictures, colour and shape to give and record information, to describe and to make sense of their own and others' experiences. 6. Use books and ICT (software and the internet) for enjoyment and as a source of information.

Aims	Learning goals
Aim 4 Children will have positive attitudes towards learning and develop dispositions like curiosity, playfulness, perseverance, confidence, resourcefulness and risk-taking.	In partnership with the adult, children will: 1. Demonstrate growing confidence in being able to do things for themselves. 2. Address challenges and cope with frustrations. 3. Make decisions and take increasing responsibility for their own learning. 4. Feel confident that their ideas, thoughts and questions will be listened to and taken seriously. 5. Develop higher-order thinking skills such as problem-solving, predicting, analysing, questioning and justifying. 6. Act on their curiosity, take risks and be open to new ideas and uncertainty.

When embracing every theme individually in respect of every child and their individual skills, attitudes and abilities, it is possible to see where themes can be used in several ways that extend each child's skills. Records must be maintained to confirm that the goals are met for each child and this should be part of the curriculum review schedule for all key workers in your setting to keep you informed about the children in their care. Eventually, every child will have their own record book of their goals, the way they were achieved and how their own individual interests have been incorporated into the process. This process allows the child and the adults who care for them to review and update the child's learning in a meaningful way.

For example, a child's interests in trains could lead to many ways of to fulfilling some of the above curriculum themes. If you and your staff use thought and creativity, you will be able to meet the requirements as long as everything is recorded in the process. For example, the child can be encouraged to:

- Talk about trains and train parts.
- Talk about the geography of the train line they are on – towns stopped at, etc.
- Look at the history of trains and introduce industry concepts.
- Look at timetables of trains and use time-telling techniques to work out how long the next train will take to arrive.
- Look at the wheels on the train and see how many segments they have and thus explore the mathematics of circles and segments, etc.
- Take photographs of different trains and email them, thus using technology.
- Look at how pistons work and how trains are driven, e.g. diesel, electric.
- Look at the advantages of a train over a car in pollution terms.
- See the layout of tables, etc. and symmetry in the carriage.
- Check tunnels and bridges that are on the line and explain why one is used instead of the other.

Reviewing Curriculum Progress

Just as it is important for every setting to follow curriculum guidelines such as Aistear and to incorporate individual needs into any curriculum plan, it is also important that there is a regular review of progress once such a plan has been implemented.

Review gives an opportunity to make changes to procedures within an overall plan in ways that allow the child to move forward or to reassess the processes being used. It looks at the effects of actions taken and allows changes to be incorporated in the best interests of that individual child.

A built-in, regular and informed review process allows every staff member to have an opportunity to evaluate the effectiveness of their work with individual children, to compare their review with others in the setting and to redraw, with support (perhaps from other members of a multidisciplinary team), new directions for the children being reviewed.

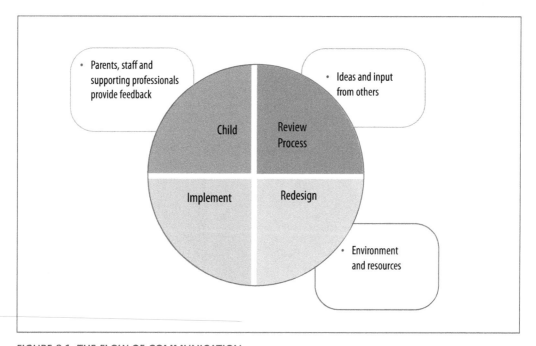

FIGURE 9.1: THE FLOW OF COMMUNICATION

As a supervisor, you should allocate time with all staff in the setting to allow inter-staff support for the curriculum activities of all team members. A child who needs an individual education plan (IEP) will need that plan to be reviewed, as a right, to ensure that they are reaching their best potential. However, this is a right that applies to all children in the setting, so a formal process should be set up so that review takes place on a regular basis and the curriculum ideas for each child are kept up to date and challenging for the child.

The process should be child centred and focus on what is being done and how it might be changed, and all stakeholders, resources and contributors should be involved. In any review process, it is important that as many factors as possible are examined and this is best done in a formal feedback procedure. Resources and environmental issues need to be re-examined for effectiveness. A review process is an opportunity for all staff to be involved, as staff who are assigned to a particular child may be experiencing something that they discover another staff member is also experiencing, and they can offer valuable support to each other. A formal meeting forum allows all staff to learn and contribute to the process in a collegial manner and to learn from others. As a supervisor, you should facilitate such progressive review sessions so that the curriculum is a central part of your team's approach to the work they do with individual children. Feedback is also supported and sought as part of a whole-team task.

TEN

Observation and Evaluation

As a supervisor, you will be involved in observing and overseeing everything that happens in the setting so that you can stand over the standards of care being given to every child. We have already discussed the need for and uses of child observations; and rationales for curriculum, intervention and support will be based on the processes of child observations that take place in the setting. The implementation of strategies to support each individual child will be based on the observations and interpretations made when comparing what is actually happening with the child and whether this fits into expected norms of behaviour and progress for that child's age and stage of development.

Child Development Theorists

The work of child development theorists is often based on their observations of how children act and react in various situations. When we agree with a theory, it may inform our activities in relation to children; but in some cases we may not have much faith in a particular theorist's work because what they say happens is different from what we actually observe – of individual children or children in general – in the setting. The faith we have in a theorist's argument can inform how we use their work in our interpretation of children's supports and achievement goals.

The following are some established theorists whose work informs the activities and the way things are done in a pre-school and, indeed, school setting.

Jean Piaget

Piaget studied the different stages in a child's development and how they view things at each stage. He identified four stages. The first, the child's earliest stage of development, which he called the sensorimotor stage, is centred on the child themselves. Understanding is based on the use of senses – taste, hearing, etc. – and movement.

The second stage is what he called the preoperational stage, where connections are made between words and objects in the environment. The third stage is described as the concrete operational stage, where differences or similarities are compared to determine whether objects are the same. The fourth and last stage is the formal operational stage, where children can imagine things, deal with abstract ideas and concepts and understand how others think and act. Piaget's theory helped develop our notion that there are certain times in children's lives when things are easier to grasp than at others and informs many of the practices used in education (e.g. introduction, experimentation and then explanation of a concept). Indeed, it informs our concept of the need for each child to develop at their own pace and to have time when they can just play and experiment.

Lev Vygotsky

Vygotsky's theory of proximal development is based on the concept that children have a level at which they will learn alone and another level at which they benefit from the help of another. He based his theory on the social aspects of being helped and staging the help as needed. This contributes to our ideas that we can get a child to gradually increase their knowledge by building on what they already know, as is done in learning support, where scaffolding is used and the task is increased as the child grasps one concept and then adds to it. The idea of testing a child to see where they are at is based on this concept of proximal learning, and the adult's support is deemed an important social element in learning.

Albert Bandura

Bandura developed his theories around the concept that children will copy what they see and how adults behave around them. He used his Bobo doll experiment to illustrate that children copy expressions, behaviours and practices. In his theories, he emphasised the need for anybody working with children to be aware that a child will do what they see an adult do, not necessarily because they like the adult , but because they see it as a type of learning opportunity without knowing the rights or wrongs of the situation. All staff must be aware of their position as role models for children in their care and act accordingly. Greeting children personally, acting responsibly and acknowledging each child's individual importance is how Bandura's theories are incorporated into the everyday workings of the pre-school setting.

John Bowlby

Bowlby's theory centred on the strength of children's attachments and the contributions that strong attachments make to their confidence and self-esteem and in turn the ability of a confident child to persevere in mastering a task. The key worker system is based on the concept of a child having one strong attachment to staff, which contributes to the child's sense of belonging, achievement, self-esteem and in turn confidence.

Jerome Bruner

Bruner identified three stages or modes of development in children: enactive, where there is physical movement; iconic, where children represent things as other objects; and symbolic, where children apply their own experiences to objects and representations. Bruner explained that children move between stages as they learn whatever they need to learn. This has informed our process of revisiting the ways in which a child grasps a concept and using different ways of explaining things in the learning process.

B.F. Skinner

Skinner looked at reinforcement and how positive reinforcement encourages children to learn more effectively. The system of giving children stars for doing positive things comes from his teachings and is widely used in settings to encourage children to behave well. This thinking is also a fundamental part of applied behaviour analysis (ABA) teaching, which is currently used with children who have autism, where small positives are acknowledged and reinforced and reactions to challenging behaviour are controlled or minimised.

Summary

The reasons we look at the work of such theorists is to see if we can apply their theories to the work we do. Theories are being developed all the time in the research of people working with children and this is another reason why you as a supervisor should keep up to date with developments in the childcare profession.

Observations

The process of observation is a learned process in childcare, but over time it becomes almost second nature to a good childcare practitioner. There are different methods for each type of activity being observed and matching the method used to the information needed to inform practice is a decision for the observer to make in consultation with you and other professionals in the setting.

At all stages, priority in the setting should be given to the reasons the observation is being made, the privacy of the setting and the child, the interpretations being made about the observations, the follow-up to the observations and the best interests of the child.

When properly carried out, observations are very informative in relation to each child in the setting and therefore these are carried out as a normal part of each child's experiences. Parents should be informed when observations are being carried out and the results should be part of the child's portfolio, which parents and other members of the team consider from time to time in a regular review of that child's progress and, where relevant, intervention needs.

As a supervisor who supports and collates the work of your staff, you will be required to oversee many different forms of observation and interpretation made by your team in relation to children in your care, and this brings with it some responsibilities.

This process is so significant in identifying the needs that some children have that the importance of accuracy and accountability cannot be overstated. Needs identified at an early stage can be easily responded to while the child is in the

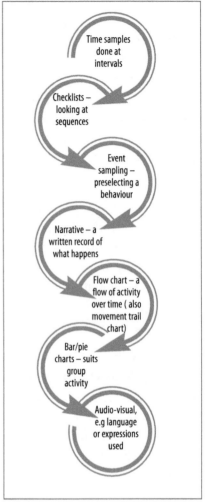

FIGURE 10.1: RANGE OF OBSERVATION METHODS

setting and while resources are available, which can help the child significantly. However, observation processes should not intrude on the development and peaceful enjoyment of the child in the setting, and staff must ensure that any observations are appropriate and timely and for the specific purpose of determining the needs of the child being observed. Therefore, staff need to be aware of what theorists have to say about children's development. As supervisor, you should keep up to date with emerging theories, which can be done through reading and, where possible, becoming familiar with recent developments in research, which can be supported through the networks we discussed in Chapter 5.

Disability and Assessment of Learning Needs

The Disability Act 2005 requires that if it is suspected that a child in the setting has a disability, they should be assessed and their individual learning needs set out. This is done via an assessment of needs report, which states how the child's needs will be met and when the process will be reviewed.

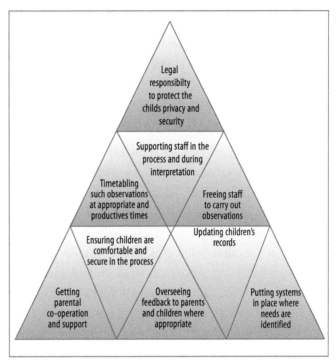

There is an increasing move towards full integration of children with disability into mainstream education, with changes being made in the school to facilitate the child's individual needs. The observations that take place in the normal running of

FIGURE 10.2: THE SUPERVISOR'S RESPONSIBILITIES IN OBSERVATION AND INTEPRETATION PROCESSES

your pre-school setting may lead to a suspicion of disability in relation to a specific child and it is your duty as supervisor to set in motion a full assessment of the child's needs. An educational psychologist can assist in this process and ascertain whether your team's suspicions are accurate. You will also be required to carry out an examination of how you propose to meet the specific requirements of that child in the setting. In some cases the HSE may initiate the assessment of needs report and in the future it is likely that you as supervisor will also need to inform and work with the Health Information and Quality Authority (HIQA) in relation to the child's care and learning needs and the provisions in the setting.

This is a developing area in childcare, but if you follow the processes (already outlined) of regularly reviewing each child's progress, this will become second nature to you and your team. At no stage can you predict what disability a child in your setting may be diagnosed with and keeping yourself up to date with each child's progress is the best way to prepare your setting and staff for whatever interventions might be needed for an individual child.

In the proper running of your setting, you may need to put extra supports in place to allow the child with a disability to reach their full potential. It may be necessary to consult with other professionals in a multidisciplinary approach to the child's needs. In such situations, conflict may occur as one professional's needs overlap with the needs of other professionals. As supervisor of the setting, you will need to negotiate in such situations and facilitate an integrated approach from everybody that highlights the child's abilities rather than the disability.

Child Observation Records

Child observation records are vital to ensure that every child reaches their best potential. The Child Care (Pre-School Services) (No. 2) (Amendment) Regulations 2006 require that records in relation to children are kept. These records should include specific information on parents, address and other administrative details, as outlined at the beginning of this book and in the regulations themselves.

Since they record children's specific identified needs, observation records inform practice and initiate interventions for to individual children. As such, they need to be kept as part of a development trail should review be necessary. However, there is a difference between repetitive observations and those that initiate intervention. Endless records of observations may distract from the more relevant ones and judgment should be exercised on the minute details that might be recorded in observations for each child and whether each needs to be kept. A child's portfolio should contain relevant observations that inform actions taken in relation to that child and these should be kept even after the child has left the setting. There is no specific period for which information must be kept, but under the Data Protection (Amendment) Act 2003, the child does have the right to request information held about them on reaching their eighteenth birthday. Obviously, records have to be stored and the setting must check that any such storage is safe, secure and suitable. Where this involves computer records, they should be encrypted to maintain privacy.

Recordkeeping and Confidentiality

As already mentioned, there are different categories of records in relation to each child in the setting:
- Specific administrative records as required by legislation and regulation.
- General and occasional records that arise in the course of a child's development.
- Assessment records that may be supplied in relation to specific children.
- Observation records as an ongoing process.
- Educational records of work produced by children.

Each type is necessary in a properly functioning and actively supportive setting. Because of each child's right to privacy, it is imperative that these records are kept in a way that protects that privacy. The Data Protection Acts 1988 and 2003 make the keeper of personal information responsible for its protection and in your setting your data protection officer is responsible for the accuracy, careful storage and protection of this information. The data protection officer will check that any inaccuracies are corrected, that those with a right to see data held about them can get copies of such records (on payment of a relevant fee set by law), and that such records are carefully disposed of when they are no longer needed.

While law directs processes to be followed in keeping information, it is also important that care is exercised as the record is being created to ensure that it is accurate and properly recorded by the childcare worker or you as the supervisor. The child may never request the information, but remember that they do have a legal right to do so when they are eighteen. More important, their right to privacy and accuracy is ongoing.

Reflective Portfolio Activity

Explain the importance of accurate recordkeeping and give five examples of records in relation to children that are held in your placement. Investigate what precautions are made in keeping such information and discuss whether you consider these to be adequate. What improvements, if any, would you make if you were the supervisor in the setting?

ELEVEN

Health and Welfare of Children

E very person working with children in an ECCE setting is required to ensure that the health and welfare of the children in their care are protected to the best of their ability. Health and welfare have many contributory factors and this chapter will address some of these.

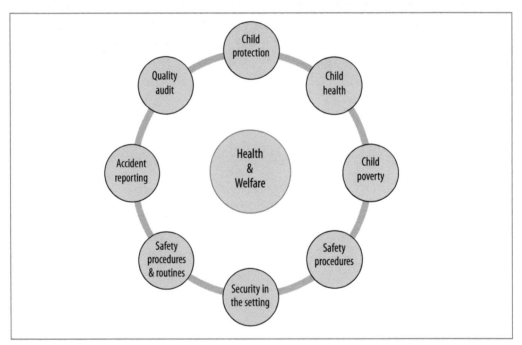

FIGURE 11.1: HEALTH AND WELFARE

Each element of the concept of health and welfare in the setting requires that a strategy or policy be developed to highlight to all stakeholders the importance of each element. As supervisor, you will be held responsible by the stakeholders for any breaches of standards in these areas, and where such breaches occur, the quality of the experience of parents, children, staff and other stakeholders will be affected.

One of the most significant ways of protecting children's health and welfare is to make everything in the setting child friendly, e.g. doors have guards that prevent little fingers getting caught, presses do not have sharp edges and plugs are inaccessible or at a height children cannot reach. These precautions relate to every piece of equipment in the setting and using the HSE inspection tool will remind you of some. This includes gates, stairs, doors, toys, equipment, kitchens, drains and any number of potential hazards that must be examined in relation to the potential they have to cause harm to a child. However, child protection also means protecting the child from harm not just from equipment and procedures, but also from people or situations that can severely harm a child.

Child Protection

The concept of protecting children is one that goes to the very heart of a child's rights under our laws and Constitution. Every setting is required to have a child protection policy in place and to review it regularly so that any precautions that need to be put in place are well thought out and understood by everybody who uses the service.

Children First: National Guidance for the Protection and Welfare of Children 2011 is the most up-to-date document on the issue of child protection in Ireland and the procedures that must be followed by anybody who suspects a child is being abused.

Children First outlines the requirements for organisations both public and private that provide services for children or that are in regular contact with children. Paragraph 1.3.1 states that such organisations must:

> … ensure best practice in the recruitment of staff or volunteers, which includes Garda vetting, taking up of references, good HR practices in interviewing, induction, training, probation and ongoing supervision and management.

There are significant implications for every supervisor in this process. It requires that the procedure for selecting staff must follow best practice. It also assumes that there is a procedure involved for all staff that includes their induction, training and ongoing supervision.

> … ensure that staff members or volunteers are aware of how to recognise signs of child abuse or neglect.

This puts the onus on you as supervisor to teach staff and volunteers to recognise signs of abuse. It assumes that training is provided to all staff and volunteers. This is absolutely as it should be to ensure the proper care and welfare protection for all children in the setting.

> ... develop guidance and procedures for staff and/or volunteers who may have reasonable grounds for concern about the safety and welfare of children involved with the organisation.

There is a presumption of ongoing guidance in this requirement, so you as supervisor need to put procedures in place that facilitate this process.

> ... identify a designated person to act as a liaison with outside agencies and a resource person to any staff member or volunteer who has child protection concerns. The designated person is responsible for reporting allegations or suspicions of child abuse to the HSE Children and Family Services or to An Garda Síochána.

The setting must have a designated person who is responsible for reporting concerns about a child and who liaises with the relevant agencies, and is also a resource person for others.

Children First defines what constitutes child abuse under four headings and also includes a definition of what constitutes a 'threshold of significant harm' in each case.

Definition of neglect

Neglect can be defined in terms of an omission, where the child suffers significant harm or impairment of development by being deprived of food, clothing, warmth, hygiene, intellectual stimulation, supervision and safety, attachment to and affection from adults, and/or medical care.

Harm can be defined as the ill treatment or the impairment of the health or development of a child. Whether it is significant is determined by the child's health and development as compared to that which could reasonably be expected of a child of similar age.

Neglect generally becomes apparent in different ways over a period of time rather than at one specific point. For example, a child who suffers a series of minor injuries may not be having their needs met in terms of necessary supervision and safety. A child whose height or weight is significantly below average may be being deprived of adequate nutrition. A child who consistently misses school may be being deprived of intellectual stimulation.

The threshold of significant harm is reached when the child's needs are neglected to the extent that their well-being and/or development are severely affected.

Definition of emotional abuse

Emotional abuse is normally to be found in the relationship between a parent/carer and a child rather than in a specific event or pattern of events. It occurs when a child's developmental need for affection, approval, consistency and security are not met. Unless other forms of abuse are present, it is rarely manifested in terms of physical signs or symptoms. Examples may include:

- The imposition of negative attributes on a child, expressed by persistent criticism, sarcasm, hostility or blaming.
- Conditional parenting in which the level of care shown to a child is made contingent on his or her behaviours or actions.
- Emotional unavailability of the child's parent/carer.
- Unresponsiveness of the parent/carer and/or inconsistent or inappropriate expectations of the child.
- Premature imposition of responsibility on the child.
- Unrealistic or inappropriate expectations of the child's capacity to understand something or to behave and control himself or herself in a certain way.
- Under- or overprotection of the child.
- Failure to show interest in or provide age-appropriate opportunities for the child's cognitive and emotional development.
- Use of unreasonable or overly harsh disciplinary measures.
- Exposure to domestic violence.
- Exposure to inappropriate or abusive material through new technology.

Emotional abuse can be manifested in terms of the child's behavioural, cognitive, affective or physical functioning. Examples of these include insecure attachment, unhappiness, low self-esteem, educational and developmental underachievement, and oppositional behaviour. The threshold of significant harm is reached when abusive interactions dominate and become typical of the relationship between the child and the parent/carer.

Definition of physical abuse

Physical abuse of a child is that which results in actual or potential physical harm from an interaction, or lack of interaction, which is reasonably within the control of a parent or person in a position of responsibility, power or trust. There may be single or repeated incidents. Physical abuse can involve:

- Severe physical punishment.
- Beating, slapping, hitting or kicking.
- Pushing, shaking or throwing.
- Pinching, biting, choking or hair-pulling.
- Terrorising with threats.
- Observing violence.
- Use of excessive force in handling.
- Deliberate poisoning.
- Suffocation.
- Fabricated/induced illness.
- Allowing or creating a substantial risk of significant harm to a child.

Definition of sexual abuse

Sexual abuse occurs when a child is used by another person for his or her gratification or sexual arousal or for that of others. Examples of child sexual abuse include:

- Exposure of the sexual organs or any sexual act intentionally performed in the presence of the child.
- Intentional touching or molesting of the body of a child, whether by a person or object, for the purpose of sexual arousal or gratification.
- Masturbation in the presence of the child or the involvement of the child in an act of masturbation.
- Sexual intercourse with the child, whether oral, vaginal or anal.
- Sexual exploitation of a child, which includes inciting, encouraging, propositioning, requiring or permitting a child to solicit for or engage in prostitution or other sexual acts. Sexual exploitation also occurs when a child is involved in exhibition, modelling or posing for the purpose of sexual arousal, gratification or sexual act, including its recording (on film, video tape or other media) or the manipulation, for those purposes, of the image by computer or other means. It may also include showing sexually explicit material to children, which is often a feature of the 'grooming' process by perpetrators of abuse.
- Consensual sexual activity involving an adult and an underage person. In relation to child sexual abuse, it should be noted that for the purposes of the criminal law, the age of consent to sexual intercourse is 17 years for both boys and girls. An Garda Síochána will deal with the criminal aspects of the case under the relevant legislation.

Source: *Children First* (Department of Children and Youth Affairs, 2011).

The three-point process outlined in *Children First* is:
1.   Considering the possibility.
2.   Looking for signs of neglect or abuse.
3.   Recording information.

These should form the basis of every setting's child protection policy, but the guidance goes a little further and outlines that in the case of vulnerable children (including those with disabilities, children who are homeless or separated from their parents or other family members and are dependent on others for their care and protection), the criteria of abuse in such cases may include 'deprivation of basic rights, harsh disciplinary regimes or the inappropriate use of medications or physical restraints'.

Children First outlines the exact procedure that must be followed when reporting a suspicion of child abuse as well as the protections afforded under the Protection for Persons Reporting Child Abuse Act 1998, where a person is protected if a report is made in good faith.

Procedures to be followed:
- Your facility must have a designated reporting person who will liaise with other agencies (this may be the HSE or even HIQA in the longer term).
- When a staff member suspects abuse, either by observation or by report from a child, they must record the details but never question the child's version. These records must be kept confidential and only shared on a need-to-know basis with other agencies.
- The designated reporting person will contact the HSE Child and Family Support Services and fill out a standard reporting form.
- Where a designated reporting person is not sure whether the course of action they are considering is correct, they are encouraged to contact the HSE and seek guidance and support.
- The designated reporting person must inform parents that the concerns about abuse are being reported and discuss the next likely actions, as well as keeping a record of discussions which take place, such as parents' reactions to such disclosure.
- The designated reporting person fills in the standard reporting form, which includes the following information to help the HSE ensure that everybody who has contact with the child in question is part of their network of investigation.
  ‣ The name, address and age of the child (or children) for whom the report is being made.
  ‣ The name of the child's school.
  ‣ The name and contact details of the person reporting the concerns.

▸ Whether the person reporting is a professional, a person working with children or a member of the public.

▸ The relationship to the child of the person making the report.

▸ A full account of what constitutes the grounds for concern in relation to the protection and welfare of the child or children, e.g. details of the allegation, incident, dates, description of any injuries, etc.

▸ The names and addresses of the parents/carers of the child or children.

▸ The names of other children in the household.

▸ The name, address and details of the person allegedly causing concern in relation to the child or children.

▸ The child's and/or parents'/carers' own views, if known and relevant.

▸ The names and addresses of other personnel or agencies involved with the child or children, e.g. GP, social worker, public health nurse, Gardaí, etc.

▸ Any other relevant information.

The HSE Children and Family Services then follow up the complaint and will investigate and work with those involved to ensure the best possible outcome for the child involved.

Having outlined the definitions of abuse, *Children First* then reminds us of the legal consequences of not reporting concerns or suspicions of child abuse under Section 176 of the Criminal Justice Act 2006, where the charge of reckless endangerment of children states:

> A person, having authority or control over a child or abuser, who intentionally or recklessly endangers a child by –
> (a) Causing or permitting any child to be placed or left in a situation which creates a substantial risk to the child of being a victim of serious harm or sexual abuse, or
> (b) Failing to take reasonable steps to protect a child from such a risk while knowing that the child is in such a situation,
> Is guilty of an offence.

The penalty for a person found guilty of this offence is a fine (no upper limit) and/or imprisonment for a term not exceeding 10 years.

These are serious consequences and are designed to ensure that every professional takes the protection of children in their care very seriously. Every organisation working with children must have a designated person who is responsible for reporting any issues to the HSE Children and Family Services or An Garda Síochána. It must also provide adequate training for staff and have policies on child protection and confidentiality.

Children First makes a distinction between professionals and non-professionals who have suspicions of child abuse – the professional should inform the parents/carers that a report is being submitted to the HSE Children and Family Services, while the non-professional may ask to remain anonymous until due process requires that they are no longer anonymous.

This distinction means that the designated reporting person and indeed all staff must be trained in how this diplomatic process should best take place, and this is the responsibility of you as supervisor. Additionally, there is a requirement for different levels of training to be undertaken by people who work with children and young people, as this is likely to be a statutory requirement in the near future. Indeed, there is a statement in *Children First* that Garda vetting, which at the moment is not a legal requirement, is soon to become so. HSE inspectors already require that all staff are Garda vetted and it is policy in all pre-school settings, so they will be well prepared when this becomes a legal responsibility.

As supervisor, you need to put proper procedures in place to ensure that all requirements, both now and in the future, in respect of children's protection are clearly understood, part of an induction process, properly trained for and continually supported.

Child Health

Children's health has a huge impact on their ability to get the most from their childhood and every setting aspires to have healthy, happy children achieving their best potential. Child health is not just about hygiene in the setting, although this is important; but it is a many-pronged concept.

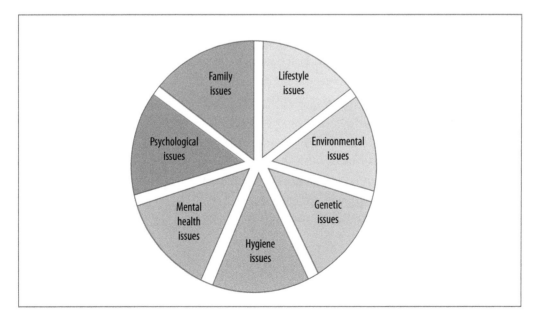

FIGURE 11.2: CHILD HEALTH

As supervisor, you will be aware of some of the issues the children in your setting bring with them on a daily basis. However, some parents might not find it easy to share with all staff in the setting. This will impact on the benefits a child gets from the setting, and where possible supports should be put in place for children to develop a sense of well-being, which can help them reach their best potential.

Hygiene issues include:

- Keeping infections under control.
- Ensuring that children who need medication regularly get it, and that a record is kept of medicines administered. It also involves a decision as to whether a child who needs medication should be in the setting in the first place and what your setting's policy is on this issue.
- Observing correct cleaning and washing routines and putting these in place so as not to put children at risk of infection.
- Ensuring that every child has received vaccinations and that correct records of such vaccinations are held in the setting, as required by the Child Care (Pre-School Services) (No. 2) (Amendment) Regulations 2006.
- Ensuring children have adequate fresh air to keep them healthy.
- Washing hands regularly and using gloves if in contact with bodily fluids.
- Keeping room temperatures at adequate levels.

Genetic issues include:

- Children can inherit conditions that may affect their health, such as cystic fibrosis, cleft palate, Down's Syndrome and arthritis.
- Genetic conditions can often be a shock to the parents and they may feel responsible for the child's condition, but this should be overcome and in pre-school settings the child should be encouraged to reach their best potential with support and acknowledgement of their condition.

Environmental issues include:

- Children who do not get adequate space to play and enough opportunities for exercise may suffer poor health.
- They may live with smog and other environmental triggers that can affect them individually, such as hay fever, asthma, etc.
- Exposure to pollutants, for example from chemical leaks, can have a lasting effect on children's health.

Lifestyle issues include:

- Lack of exercise and sedentary activities at home.
- Excessive time on the computer or in front of the TV.

- Economic pressures can be stressful for children.
- Pressure to succeed and be the best they can: some parents put too much pressure on children in the race to succeed.
- Families may have cultural beliefs or customs that can affect children's health.

Family issues include:
- Perhaps a family member is sick and needs more support.
- Sibling rivalry can impact on a child's sense of well-being.
- Parents may be going through turbulent times and this can impact on the child.
- There may be no family support systems in place for the child if the family has had to move to find a job or affordable housing.
- The family may be immigrants who find it hard to settle in the country or who have little support.
- Family units differ and have different effects on children.

Psychological issues include:
- Children may engage in potentially harmful behaviours as a result of boredom, learning difficulties or other factors that must be investigated.
- Some psychological conditions may cause children to be impulsive, which can put them at risk.
- Parents' psychological problems can affect a child's health.

Mental health issues include:
- Children can suffer from depression at any stage in their lives.
- Seasonal affective disorder (SAD) can affect children.
- Trauma can affect a child's ability to fully engage in the setting or to trust people.

These examples give an indication of the many factors that can affect a child's health. The job of the supervisor and staff in the setting is to ensure that, in so far as is possible, no issue is overlooked in determining the cause of any health issues in relation to a child. Getting to the bottom of the causes of ill health and acknowledging any contributory factors are necessary for a child to engage fully in the setting. Procedures must be put in place to protect the health of children, such as ensuring that all children who are sick do not attend the setting so as not to pass on infectious diseases. This is a job that changes as different children come into the setting and will require good information and records to be available to you as a supervisor. It also requires you to try to find the contributory factors of each child's well-being in your setting.

Child Poverty

Poverty can impact on children's health and their engagement in the setting. Poverty is about not being able to afford the basics of life with the means a person has at their disposal. In Ireland, where we have a well-developed system of social welfare, there is a presumption that child poverty does not exist at the same level as it might in countries where absolute poverty can be caused by famine or other disasters. More common in Ireland is relative poverty, which means that a person's income is lower than the average. Strictly applying the definition of relative poverty does not give a complete view of the factors that could be at play in a child's life. We may never know the full picture, but there are some specific factors that might influence the income families have at any given time and thus the likelihood that they will experience poverty.

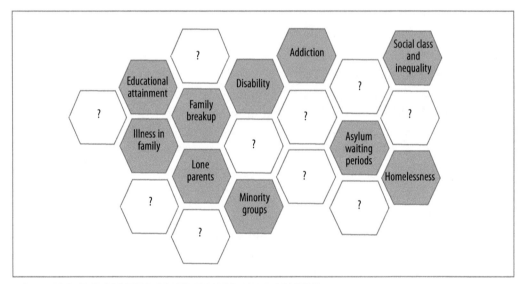

FIGURE 11.3: FACTORS THAT CONTRIBUTE TO CHILD POVERTY

Whatever the causes, there can be numerous effects on a child:
- Isolation and not being accepted by peers.
- Inability to engage fully because they feel different.
- Poor health.
- Embarrassment.
- Poor self-esteem.
- Poor housing and lack of space to work or play.
- Hunger.
- Behavioural issues due to feeling different.
- Poor clothing.

- Lack of freedom, as they must work rather than play.
- Poor attainment, as they have bigger issues than education on their mind.

Putting strategies in place to overcome poverty for children can dramatically change their potential life outcomes and every supervisor should examine how they can provide for children who are experiencing either consistent or temporary poverty. Organising book lending schemes in pre-school settings or having parties in the setting can help a child's self-esteem. There are agencies, such as St Vincent de Paul, that can help when families suffer from periods of poverty, and these may be part of the network in a setting: they can be discreetly contacted if a child is thought to be experiencing poverty for whatever reason. Discretion is important in any such interventions, and as supervisor you must ensure that the problem is not overlooked, as poverty can affect the child's life for many years after the issues that caused the poverty are dealt with.

Providing leaflets for parents in the setting is a good way to give information to parents who experience difficulties from time to time. This allows the parent to maintain their privacy and at the same time find out where they can get advice and assistance.

> ### Reflective Portfolio Activity
> Name six factors that can cause stress in a child's life and discuss the effects of each on the child's ability to engage in a setting. Design leaflets for the setting giving information on each of the factors you have chosen and showing where advice and assistance can be found.

Safety Procedures

The procedures used to ensure children's safety while in the setting are hugely important to the well-being of every child. Nothing should be taken for granted and constant vigilance is needed to ensure that all staff follow procedures that will keep children safe. There are three factors that contribute to an effective approach to safety procedures.

Forethought

Thinking about what might cause harm in the setting requires that you examine and record every procedure that takes place in the minutest detail to see when harm is likely to occur.

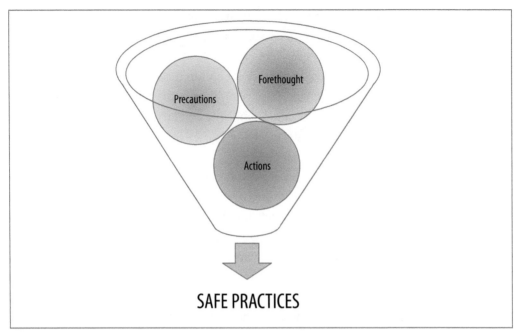

SAFE PRACTICES

FIGURE 11.4: FACTORS THAT CONTRIBUTE TO SAFETY PRACTICES

Precautions

Put in place ways of doing things that will prevent any possible harm that could arise. This means that everybody should be informed and trained about the methods they use and how they may be modified.

Actions

Once the above steps have been taken, everybody in the setting should agree on the correct way of avoiding whatever has the potential to cause the harm you wish to avoid. An example of this is the procedure your setting uses when children are being brought to the toilet. Every setting must have a written procedure to make sure that everybody knows what should happen so that dignity and safety for all are taken into account.

This three-step process requires constant review to check that agreed procedures are followed. It applies to all activities in the setting and can save children, staff and management unnecessary stress.

> ### Reflective Portfolio Activity
> Every setting has different procedures for when children wish to go out in the playground. Look at the procedures in your setting and discuss how you feel they might be improved. Discuss the reasons why you would make the changes you suggest and how they would make things better for staff or children in the setting.

Security

Principle 8 of Síolta states that practitioners must oversee 'a safe and secure setting which protects a child's welfare'. To implement this principle, a supervisor must put in place the security a child centre requires and then oversee the process. Security issues in childcare are numerous because of the vulnerability of the children in the setting. However, security has a twofold meaning in childcare: safety-related security; and the security a child feels in any given situation.

The security issues surrounding physical access to the setting are vital to protect children while they are in the setting. Owners and supervisors in any childcare setting must not endanger children (bearing in mind the crime of reckless endangerment of a child in the Criminal Justice Act 2006) and have a duty of care to put systems in place that protect children. As an employer, it is also necessary to protect staff and visitors to the setting.

These precautions include:

- Safe and secure locks on entrances and doors.
- Ensuring that any issues relating to access to the child in the family situation are adhered to, e.g. where there are restrictions or care orders in relation to a child.
- Adequate records are held on emergency contacts and people who may collect children from the setting at any time.
- Access codes should be regularly changed and proper procedures must be stated so that all staff are aware of precautions needed at doorways.
- When children are in outdoor areas, there should be a system of supervision that ensures they do not come to harm.
- All staff must be Garda vetted regularly – once is not enough. There should be a regular review period within which staff should be vetted again to check that no charges have been made.
- Check boundaries regularly to make sure that they are robust.
- Ensure that doors and windows in the setting have fixtures that protect children from trap injuries.

- Child/adult ratios must be maintained in the setting so that children are adequately supervised.
- Toys and equipment are regularly cleaned, tested and, if required, replaced.
- Children have adequate room to move around. This must take account of any restrictions in movement that might be occasioned by disability, or access restrictions that may be imposed by illness or additional needs.
- Proper supervision systems are in place to ensure that children are protected when on educational or social outings.
- Keeping records of visitors to the setting and the times of access and egress.
- Proper maintenance of the building and fixtures to ensure that users of the premises do not come to any harm.
- Policies and procedures for any risks identified as potential causes of harm in the setting.

The above list is not exhaustive. Most of these precautions will be covered by specific policies and procedures in the setting that will outline practices to be followed to minimise any risks identified.

Safety Procedures and Routines

Síolta's Standard 5 states that 'all interactions in children's lives, whether with other children or with other adults, should be supported by policies and be child centred and child enabling'. Ensuring that children have a sense of safety in the setting and feel that their needs are being met forms a big part of their well-being. This allows a child to feel comfortable enough to achieve their best potential, as they are less worried about the possibilities of things causing them harm and can concentrate on doing what they need to do. Feeling safe and acknowledged in the setting has many benefits for a child: a child who feels secure will thrive and with support will learn to overcome obstacles and to help others too.

As supervisor, you must emphasise to your team and support staff the importance of each child's unique place in the setting so that they engage in a meaningful way with each individual child and their unique set of needs. A child with a disability will gain more from a setting where people are aware of the efforts they make to achieve the same milestones as other children, while a child with unique talents will thrive where they receive adequate challenges to meet their needs while still enjoying their childhood. Just saying it should happen is not enough, and Síolta's goal is to ensure that adequate procedures are in place to make this happen. This must be borne in mind as an ongoing process that should be regularly reviewed and should be supported by structures that promote the work that is undertaken.

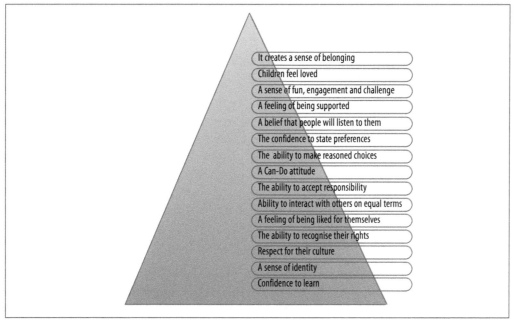

FIGURE 11.5: BENEFITS OF FEELING SAFE AND ACKNOWLEDGED

Putting a key worker system in place can facilitate an individualised approach to each child's needs and the support structures that will allow a child to scaffold their learning and care needs to become the most productive and fulfilled person they can be. Not all children have perfect backgrounds, and occasionally the time a child spends in a safe and secure environment may be the only time that child can feel a sense of esteem, which will stand to them in later life. In such cases, all staff should be motivated to ensure that the child gets as many opportunities as possible to achieve their full potential. A key worker system also fits in with Principle 5 of Síolta, which states that the child should be encouraged to build 'meaningful positive relationships that support the child'.

A sense of knowing what is likely to happen next also helps a child to feel secure and safe in the setting. Setting routines during the day means that activities are balanced in terms of challenge and need, such as having a nap at the best time for that child or eating meals at times that ensure that the child has adequate food to provide them with energy and nutrients for their needs. All of this takes planning for the individual child and this is a big part of the supervisor's job as part of the team.

Every routine will vary depending on the age and stage of the child. Babies may spend more time asleep in their day than a Montessori child, as their need for sleep is greater. Stimulating activities should encourage interaction at the level the child is at, while ensuring they have adequate play, fresh air and nurturing means the child develops through each stage of their development with the care and encouragement needed to feel a sense of belonging.

> *Reflective Portfolio Activity*
> Look at the children in your setting and list the things that are undertaken in the setting that acknowledge the individual child's needs and incorporate them into their daily or weekly routine in a way that supports that child to reach their full potential. Also discuss what challenges this poses and how the challenges are overcome by the staff in the setting you are observing.

Accident Reporting

Accountability and responsibility go hand in hand in any pre-school setting where all childcare workers act *in loco parentis* (in the place of the parents). This concept and the commitment of everybody to the best interests of each individual child in the setting requires that a supervisor must have policies and procedures to deal with accidents.

There is often fear surrounding the admission that an accident might happen in the setting and the possibility of bad publicity, but this should be tempered with the goal of making the setting the best possible place for every child. Every accident must be reported, no matter how small, as the possibility of harm to a child is present in every accident, whether dramatic or trivial, and failure to report and take responsibly leaves the setting liable to a claim of abuse of the child.

Part of the responsibility of everyone in the setting is to include children and parents in consultations, and reporting accidents falls into this category. Small knocks that might take place in the ordinary activities of the setting, such as a toddler banging their head on a table because it just happens to be at their height, or tripping over their own feet, should not be regular occurrences if the child is being looked after and supported in their endeavours to walk, but they can and do happen. In such cases, it may be enough to explain to the parent in person and in writing in an accident book how the accident happened and how it was dealt with. There should be a record kept of such instances, as they may lead to more serious consequences depending on the child; one child may fall and not be hurt, while another might sustain serious harm from the same mishap. A consistent process of recording accidents must be kept up to date and available for everybody to consult, and it should be reviewed regularly to see if things can be put in place to avoid the accidents that are being reported.

Knowing what was done following an accident can provide doctors and other medical personnel with further information where necessary. The accident record will detail the steps taken and assist a careful analysis in the best interests of the child. Every setting must have their own reporting procedure (part of the inspection process by the HSE), but every procedure should cover some basic points, such as:

- The name of the child.
- The date and time of the incident.
- Where the accident happened.
- What actually happened.
- The nature of the injury suffered by the child.
- Who was present when the accident happened.
- What actions were taken and why.
- If first aid was administered and if so, how.
- Whether a doctor/hospital was consulted and what advice was given.
- Whether parents were phoned, consulted or informed and whether they gave instructions.
- What happened next.

All these points relate to accountability – you should not try to avoid responsibility for the accidents that happen in the setting. It is much more important to ensure that the child is well cared for and recovers quickly.

Quality Audits

An audit is about looking at every process in the setting and examining whether or not it is meeting the targets set for it. If not, the quality audit requires you to examine ways in which things or processes can be improved and how to go about doing so. You are the person who will be responsible for setting the standards against which your setting will be audited, and these standards should follow the standards set out in the HSE inspection tool (see Chapter 4). There must be a commitment to the process from the whole setting, which requires honesty in the examination of the way things are done. This process requires you as supervisor to be up to date with developments in relation to standards in childcare and to know how these are best implemented in the setting. However, this is not an isolated job. All your stakeholders have a part to play in the process, as they need to make you aware of things that might need to be addressed and they can also be a valuable resource in making things happen.

Where there is an imbalance between expected outcomes and resources available, then you as supervisor must commit to putting in the resources needed (even if this requires funding). Where standards are not being met, you must undertake remedial actions dictated by those standards, and where personnel need training or further development, you must provide time for such training as well as sourcing the type of training that best fits your specific needs.

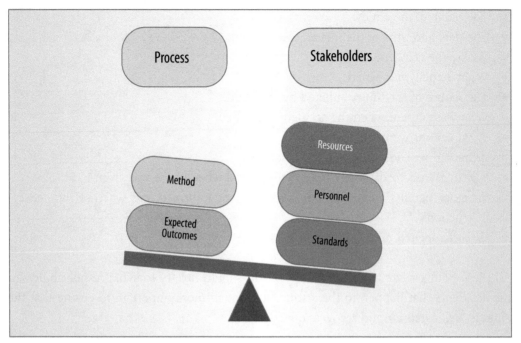

FIGFIGURE 11.6: MAINTAINING QUALITY IS A BALANCING ACT

Quality auditing means looking at:

- The way things are done.
- Who does them.
- The standards being achieved.
- How efficiently things get done.
- What might improve results.
- How to go about doing what needs to be done.

Everything needs to be included, and this can only be done effectively if you are well informed and fully involved in the processes, either in person or through delegation or as part of a team. Quality audits are challenging for everybody. How they are approached can reveal much about your management style. You will be best placed to ensure that the process produces the results you need to run an efficient setting that meets everybody's needs, but especially those of the children in the setting.

TWELVE

Organisation

Philosophies

As we have already seen, many settings have their own unique philosophies that guide the mission statement and the ways things happen in the setting. However, the philosophy of the setting is not just about the learning or care philosophies, although they may set the tone for how things happen. Much more important, the way things are organised and supported can determine much about what happens in the setting from day to day. The philosophy of a setting is the basis of its goals and plans.

- Where the philosophy of the setting is focused on **equality**, people of all abilities will be welcome and you would expect to see resources in place to facilitate approachability. Everything will revolve around inclusion and taking part, whatever your level.
- Where the philosophy is about **standards of excellence** being achieved at all costs, there will be a focus on processes and methods. This can sometimes impact on the interactions in the setting, where people-centred is replaced with process-centred.
- Where the philosophy is about **caring and nurturing**, children and others involved in the setting can expect that support and personal growth will probably be the first priority on a daily basis and that plans or routines in the setting will focus on the care needs of each person in the setting.
- There are also settings whose philosophy is to run them like a business in such a way that it makes a profit. In such settings, things may be done with an **economic** concentration, with extras being charged for at commercial levels.
- Some settings may also have an **academic** philosophy, which puts an emphasis on academic achievements and the goal of learning.

Different philosophies can affect the style of management and thereby the experiences of everybody in the setting. The important thing to remember is that these examples depict different philosophies, not different standards. Standards must be achieved no matter what the philosophy is, but the way in which this happens is dictated or influenced by the philosophy. Philosophies affect how goals are set and reviewed, and in turn the planning influences the impact of change in the setting.

Openness

The concept of openness in an organisation relates to the setting's ability to welcome outsiders, encourage input, be transparent in procedures, value opinions, be receptive to change, explorative of challenge and interact with its environment.

Every ECCE setting purports to be open and welcoming, but there are often subtle messages in the way things are organised (e.g. restrictive admission policies) that suggest that openness is not the reality, which can mean that opportunities and challenges are being overlooked. An open setting is one that has a dynamic nature that is reflected in the activities and achievements of the children.

There may be barriers to openness that are unintentional, and where they arise they should be challenged in the best interests of the children in the setting.

- **Uncertainty:** Not knowing what might be encountered and how it may change the way things are currently done. This will create a setting that eventually closes in on itself and stunts its own growth potential.
- **Feeling threatened:** This may happen when people put their own self-interests before those of the children in the setting. It makes for an insular and protective setting where power becomes the focus instead of children.
- **Different and challenging interests:** Staff have a natural lifespan in a setting, and where the setting has concentrated on only one person's interests and facilitating that person, there may be a void after that staff member has moved on. In such cases the setting will be at a severe loss if it has not planned to be open to change and innovation.

Where individual children's needs must be met, it can be very limiting for a child if a setting has a less than open approach, as the child will be restricted in the choices they have available to them and the challenges they can negotiate, as envisaged by Principle 7 of Síolta ('ensuring the child enjoys an enriching, quality and stimulating environment'). Even in situations where multi-agency involvement is needed in a child's life, for whatever reason, an open setting will allow better interaction and sharing of resources and expertise so that the child can achieve the best outcome possible. Barriers such as those discussed above must be overcome and this requires training, listening, good supervision that is enabling, and support for the opinions of everyone in the setting, including the children themselves.

Writing Policies and Procedures

As we have mentioned throughout this book, there is a requirement under the Child Care (Pre-School Services) (No. 2) (Amendment) Regulations 2006 to have written policies and procedures for the way things are done in the setting. Writing policies is a necessary part of any setting. Similarly, Standard 14 of Síolta on Identity and Belonging requires that pre-school settings 'promoting positive identities and a strong sense of belonging require clearly defined policies, procedures and practice that empower every child and adult to develop a confident self- and group identity, and to have a positive understanding and regard for the identity and rights of others'. Much more important than just writing the policies and procedures, then, is getting a commitment from all stakeholders that the policies and procedures of the setting will become working live documents that promote and support confidence and a sense of belonging.

 A policy is a statement of the rules or the stance taken on a particular practice or activity in the setting. For example, 'children's personal toys should not be brought to the setting' might be a policy.

 The procedure follows from the policy – in this case, it sets out what will happen if the child brings their personal toys to the setting. It usually does this by explaining the reason or justification for not allowing the toys and setting out the steps that will be taken when the policy is not upheld.

 Approached in this way, it's easy to think of the various policies and procedures you need and how to go about writing them. While everybody has a part to play in a quality audit (see Chapter 11), they have just as much a part to play in writing the setting's policies and procedures.

 Taking as an example the policy above of a child not bringing their personal toys to the setting, the process to be followed in writing a procedure for this would include the following.

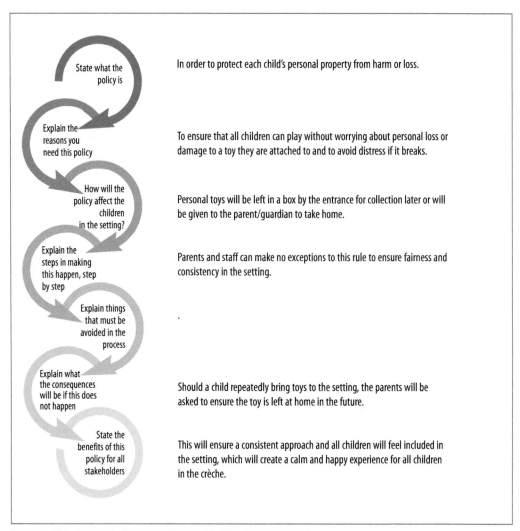

FIGURE 12.1: STEPS IN WRITING POLICIES AND PROCEDURES

This process, which might at first glance appear simplistic, is an excellent way to get a first draft of any procedure once you have stated the policy. There will be some policies that will be dictated by laws and regulations and these may include more detail, but they will follow the same format. In such policies and procedures, you need to state the law being adhered to as one of the reasons for having the policy and procedure in the first place.

An important part of being able to stand over your policies and procedures is that they are:

- **Realistic:** They should be easily understood and practical in the setting.
- **Inclusive:** They should involve every member of the setting and not exclude anybody.

- **Fair:** It should be easy for people to see why they are needed and to understand how they will improve things.
- **Consultative:** All stakeholders must be included in the process and their views should be sought, which means that they buy into the process too.
- **Applicable:** There should be no barriers that you are aware of to the policy being implemented in the setting.
- **Reviewed:** All procedures should be reviewed regularly to check that they are still relevant.
- **Distributed** to all stakeholders in the setting, as only then can you be sure that everybody knows, understands and implements them.

Every process in the setting should have its own policy and procedure to describe the steps that should be taken and why they should be taken. New ones should be drafted when a review of actions indicates adjustments are needed. This ensures that the setting is up to date and working at a standard that allows the children to receive a service that meets their needs as well as ensuring that there is ongoing standards maintenance. This fulfils Standard 14 of Síolta.

Some of the policies that should be in place will be dictated by law, others by regulations and others by practical needs. Some may be incorporated into others, e.g. the policy above could be incorporated into a general policy about toys and equipment use. Whatever the reason for the policies and procedures you write for your setting, there are some benefits of having them in place, which include:

- Providing for consistency in the setting.
- Assisting the ease of operation of the setting.
- Ensuring equality of approach to issues that arise.
- Avoiding problems of interpretation.
- Being culturally consistent.
- Ensuring that everybody (staff, visitors, children and other stakeholders) knows what to expect.
- Ensuring the safety, welfare and well-being of everybody in the setting.

Because running a pre-school setting involves so many different variables, there are many policies and procedures that can be written, including:

Confidentiality of documents (*Children First* 2011)	Toys and equipment
	Human resources
Child Protection (Child Care Act 1991)	Dignity at work
Inclusion	Accident reporting
Diversity and culture	Photography and videos
Bullying and behaviour management	Garda vetting and references
Recruitment and training	Food safety
Curriculum, learning and care	Hygiene
Observation and assessment	Violence
Collection of children	Travel with children
Outings	Outdoor supervision
Admissions and access	HACCP (hazard analysis and critical control point) and food handling
Security and notification	
Administration of medicines	Nappy changing and toileting
Exclusion for illness and infections	Hazards, health, safety and welfare
Head lice	Smoking
Equality	Staff supervision
Fire safety	

This list is not exhaustive but is relevant to most settings. The important thing is not to be afraid of writing policies. If you are in doubt as to where to start, you should request copies of other policies/procedures from others in your network and use them as indicators of how to proceed. In all instances you must consult all the stakeholders so that their voices are heard and interpreted and so that they are included in the final decisions made where relevant.

Staff Selection and Interviewing

One of the most important policies in every ECCE setting relates to staff selection and interviewing. Clear guidelines regarding Garda vetting are included in the Child Care (Pre-School Services) (No. 2) (Amendment) Regulations 2006 and in *Children First* 2011, which stipulate that every childcare worker should be Garda vetted and all references should be verified.

However, there are other issues in relation to staff selection and interviewing that you as supervisor need to consider (See Chapter 13 for more interviews).

Job description

Part of the process of finding the right staff member is drawing up a fair and comprehensive description of what the job will entail. It is just as important to be aware of what the job does *not* entail. In preparing the job description, the skills necessary for the job should be listed, and the tasks that have to be performed by the person doing the job may dictate some or all of these skills.

The person may need to have certain qualifications (which should be specified) for the job as well as certain personality traits, which should also be described, e.g. whether they are required to be autonomous or self-starters or to work under supervision or to be able to work well with others.

Any number of criteria may come from the use of the 5 Ws described earlier in this book (who, what, where, when, why: see Chapter 5). The robustness of this process will act as a filter for the person thinking of applying for the job, as it will help them decide if they would like the type of job described. This description is also important for the contract that will be drawn up later with the successful candidate.

At this stage you should rank the importance of any criteria you wish the ideal candidate to have, which will be useful in the next stages of the process. An example of this might be:

1. Two years' full-time post-qualification experience.
2. Experience in the Baby Room.
3. Capable of working on own initiative as well as working under supervision.
4. First aid certificate and manual handling certificate awarded in the last two years.
5. Ability to interact with parents and work in a multidisciplinary team.

This process helps you to write your advert for the job in clear and unambiguous language so that an applicant knows exactly what is being looked for. If you use words like 'must have', 'essential' or 'necessary', the message in the advert will be clear.

Shortlisting

Once the job has been advertised (this can be done in many ways: on websites, forums, colleges, employment offices, in newspapers or childcare magazines), your job will then be to decide who to interview from the applicants.

A handy way of deciding how you will select those for interview is based on the ranking you gave to every point you highlighted in the job description (you can allocate a point for each criterion satisfied, e.g. 1 if they have it and 0 if they don't). You can then set a base score below which you will not interview the candidate.

You should have a checklist of the points you used, which could look like the following.

TABLE 12.1

No.	Criteria	Mark
1	Two years' full-time post-qualification experience	1
2	Experience in the Baby Room	0
3	Capable of working on own initiative as well as working under supervision	1
4	First aid certificate and manual handling certificate awarded in the last two years	1
5	Ability to interact with parents and work in a multidisciplinary team	1
	TOTAL MARKS	4

Using a process like this can eliminate many of the applications you receive and allows you to use a transparent method to shortlist for interview. Such a process can save considerable time.

Interview preparation

When preparing for the interview process, you should use the same grid (Table 12.1), which allows you to connect all parts of the selection process. If you have particular preferences for one of the criteria, you can now weight that criterion by giving it extra points. For example, if you think a specific type of experience is better than another and want to show that this is important, you could, say, attach a 30% ranking to it. If first aid and manual handling certificates are high on the list, you could rank them at 25%, leaving a total of 45% to be divided between the other points.

Next, you should devise questions that determine the suitability of the candidate. Use a number of specifically pointed questions, which have a focus based on the ranking you gave to each criterion. Inform all candidates of the need for Garda vetting and follow through on any references given to check that you have all possible information at your disposal when making a final selection.

Equality of interview

Every candidate has a right to be treated equally in any interview process, which means that every interview should be transparent and recordable. Using the method described above allows you to include specific questions that focus on the weighting of each criterion. Other questions and conversations will be included in the interview, but you will be able to create a uniformity of interview by using your selected questions. Generating a selection of questions (using the grid and criteria throughout) will allow you to focus on the job description you started with.

You are now ready to notify the shortlisted candidates of the time of their interview. You also have an approximation of how long each interview will take, which allows you to calculate a suitable timeframe for the process that fits into your timetable as well as that of any other person who is included on an interview panel.

Feedback

Every candidate is entitled to know how he or she did at the interview and asking for feedback where you have been unsuccessful is now a normal part of the interview process. The above system allows you to clearly identify where a candidate fell short and to inform them of the system used and how they scored. An unsuccessful candidate this time may be successful next time if they have received constructive feedback and in time may become a valuable member of your team. More important, you will have a robust process that assists you in fulfilling Standard 11 of Síolta, which states that 'practising in a professional manner requires that individuals have skills, knowledge, values and attitudes appropriate to their role and responsibility within the setting. In addition, it requires regular reflection upon practice and engagement in supported, ongoing professional development.'

At the end of the selection process you should have chosen the most appropriate candidate for the job you described and for which you placed particular value on specific skill sets. You are now in a position to introduce that person to your setting knowing that they are up to a standard you value, provided their references stack up and they have appropriate Garda vetting clearance.

Teamwork

Organising teams in the ECCE sector requires a disciplined evaluation of everybody's contribution to the setting, which will be based on your observational skills as a supervisor, to find people who can work together with complementary skills in the best interests of the children in their care. There are various ways you can select teams in the ECCE setting and the effectiveness of the team may reflect the thought process that goes into that selection:

- **Finding specifically qualified people for each team:** An example of this may be that you require every team in the setting to have one person with a qualification that includes arts and craft for children. Or you may want each team to have somebody who speaks a specific language, such as Irish or French or another relevant language. Additionally, you may want somebody with a maturity that can command a presence and lead a team (however, maturity and team leadership skills should not be considered synonymous). As supervisor, you may be the best person to pick such a team, as you know the individual characteristics and experiences of each staff member.
- **Random groupings** who will develop over time into a team structure with training and interactions such as teamwork. This is a more risky selection process: while there may be a cohesive team after the training, you also run the risk of everybody finding out that they cannot work with each other.

- **Multidisciplinary teams** may be formed for groups of children who need the experience of each member of the team, such as occupational therapists, speech therapists, psychologists, psychiatrists, play therapists, etc. These teams allow for a concentration on the needs of the children in their care and this may require qualifications beyond that of a childcare worker.

There are many combinations of people who make up a team in the setting and the efficiency of the team will be discussed in another chapter. How you view your own role in the process (facilitator, overseer, team member or expert outsider) will impact on the workings of the teams you create.

THIRTEEN

Professional Practice

The level of professionalism in any ECCE setting is a measure of good management and leadership. It is shown when staff, children and all stakeholders feel comfortable with their roles and contributions to the setting and when parents, children, staff and management work together in a seamless way for the benefit of the children in the setting. While it may appear to be a seamless process, it is made up of smaller contributing factors that form part of the fabric of a fully functional, progressive and informed setting.

Qualifications

Qualifications and professional practice go hand in hand. Having the skills to make informed decisions on the developmental stages of a child and the skills to evaluate the next steps needed in that development is a process that ensures that every child can reach their full potential.

In Ireland, we are going through a process of change in relation to qualifications. Until fairly recently, it was not necessary for everybody working in childcare to have a relevant qualification (which is not to say that experience was not relevant) until the introduction of the formal ECCE scheme and funding. For settings that signed up for this government initiative, there was a requirement that over a reasonable timeframe, staff would achieve a FETAC Level 5 qualification in childcare to work with children in the ECCE setting, while owners and supervisors would have a FETAC Level 6 qualification. This has now been formalised following the publication in November 2010 of *A Workforce Development Plan for the Early Childhood Care and Education Sector in Ireland* by the Department of Education and Skills. Requirements can now be mapped as follows.

TABLE 13.1: QUALIFICATION CLASSIFICATION IN THE ECCE SECTOR

Occupational profile from the model framework	NFQ level	Comment
Basic practitioner	Level 4	This may equate to a major award or the best fit may be a minor or special purpose award at that level.
Intermediate practitioner	Level 5	This would generally equate to a major award (FETAC Level 5 Certificate), or to a minor or a special purpose award.
Experienced practitioner	Level 6	This would generally equate to a FETAC Advanced Certificate at Level 6.
Advanced practitioner	Level 7/8	This would equate to at least an ordinary bachelor's degree.
Expert practitioner	Level 8/9	This would equate to at least an honours bachelor's degree.

This is an emerging categorisation process and there are still decisions to be made in relation to recognising prior learning, but it is a working start that clearly sets out the levels at which qualifications must be attained. Equivalency for qualifications other than FETAC are facilitated and the results are already evident in the ability of every ECCE setting to deliver a quality childcare service that is well informed on the needs of all children.

Under the Child Care (Pre-School Services) (No. 2) (Amendment) Regulations 2006, every qualification must be recorded and held on file in the setting and such information must be available for HSE inspection. The onus is on the provider of the ECCE service to ensure that staff are suitably qualified and that all certificates, including equivalencies, are available for inspection.

Additionally, staff need to have qualifications such as hazard analysis and critical control point (HACCP), first aid, manual handling and others that may relate to children in the setting and their individual needs. These qualifications will also need to be kept on file in a format that is set out in the regulations. Never underestimate the value of displaying the qualifications of all staff in the setting, as it can be very reassuring for parents to see that all the staff are fully qualified. They will also be able to see that qualification requirements change over time and that your setting monitors such developments.

Training

Keeping staff up to date and informed about such a dynamic sector will be an ongoing process since developments in the sector are continuous, as evidenced by the *Children First* requirement that professionals working in childcare should have training in child protection. While this was not an unexpected development, it is evidence of the need to keep up to date with developments in the sector.

There are various approaches to training for any organisation, as follows.

In service

Specialised providers in the sector may provide training and this can be done over a period of time and at a level that is consistent across the sector. Therefore, staff do not need to leave work to carry out the training and you as supervisor can provide development opportunities that are of a high quality and recognised as being fit for purpose.

In house

Access to seminars, speakers and other training opportunities for staff to develop their skills can be provided by keeping informed about events happening in your area and consulting with childcare committees you have access to. This gives staff a feeling of continual development as well as allowing management potential in your staff to be maximised.

Exchanges

Seeing developments in other childcare settings can often be an enlightening experience for any childcare worker. Visiting Forest Schools or settings with some other cultural emphasis will help staff put their own skills to the test and challenge their own understanding of working with children from different backgrounds. Similarly, inviting other practitioners to your setting may motivate your staff to feel proud of their own achievements in the ways they work with children in your setting.

Networking

We have already discussed the value of networking for supervisors (see Chapter 5), but this is also an important source of sector knowledge for all staff in the setting. Subscribing to newsletters and e-zines from organisations in the childcare industry is a good way of providing affordable training on developments in the sector for all staff. Also, online training may be available from reputable contacts who have embraced the technological sphere, and these can be cost- and time-effective.

Whatever type of training you decide to put in place for the team in your setting (which should be based on your assessment of the skills required for the job), it is important that it is relevant, timely, professional and sufficient for the needs of your staff.

Staff Selection

We have already seen the grid you can develop as part of your recruitment process and shown how the job description can become an important part of the selection process (see Chapter 12). However, there are other considerations that can form part of the final selection process for staff, including:

- **Best fit for the children in the setting:** There may be children who have specific requirements in relation to their care and this may become part of the weighting at the interview.
- **Best fit for the team in the setting:** As supervisor, you know the dynamics of your team, the philosophy of the setting and the mission statement, which all play a part in the selection of staff to fit in with the existing team.
- **Addition to the skill sets in the team:** This may be about a vision of where the setting wishes to be in the future and building changing visions of the skill sets needed to make that move possible.
- **Replacement of experience:** There may be older staff who will be retiring in the near future, so your selection may be based on the need for an experienced replacement.

As supervisor, you will have reasons for looking for particular traits in new staff and you will approach the interview process with these in mind. As a result, you may need to look at the grid you developed for the job description and (in the interests of transparency) allocate marks for each point you are looking for in the prospective employee. This then gives you a total mark that each candidate can attain and will enable you to rank candidates on their achievement at interview in a fair and consistent manner. However, in order to be sure that you do get everything you can from each candidate, you need to ask some relevant and informative questions that are not just about qualifications so that you can get a good overall impression of the person behind the qualification.

Questions should be:

- **Probing:** Check that they have whatever experience they say they have.
- **Exploring:** Ask them what they think they can offer you – this lets you see what their vision is of your setting and it is a good way to see how others think your setting could be improved.
- **Consultative:** Asking about developments in the sector will indicate what views they might have about the way the sector is heading. This may or may not fit in with the vision you have of the sector.
- **Worst case:** Asking a prospective employee about the worst thing that ever happened to them in a setting (remember, in our example we asked for two years' experience) will indicate what challenges they have faced, how they dealt with them and, more important, what they consider to be a challenge.
- **Interests and hobbies:** This usually gives you an insight into a person's interests

in life and may even indicate a deep immersion in one hobby that might interfere with their ability to give a full-time commitment to the job. Alternatively, their interests may offer opportunities for advancement of some initiative you have put in place in the setting.

The above types of question will give you a good indication of the suitability of the interviewee for the job in question. Giving the interviewee the opportunity to ask questions may also indicate what they are worried about in relation to your setting. Interviewees often ask about money and this can sometimes be an indicator that this is their only motivation: not ideal in childcare, which is very much a caring profession. However, no one question is going to help you select your ideal candidate and a combination of answers and insights will indicate whether you feel the person is suited to childcare.

Staff Appraisal

A staff appraisal is a formal assessment of how you feel a staff member is performing their job at a particular point in time. For a staff member who is on probation, this can be an important part of the probation process, as it lets the employee know how you feel they are performing and how you think they might need to improve some aspects of their performance. Where an appraisal system has been in place during a staff member's probation and no improvements have been seen, it may be a reason to terminate their employment before or after the completion of the probation period. Once properly recorded and transparent, the process of continual appraisal can form a defence for a decision that might be appealed.

Every employee should regularly get feedback on their performance to ascertain if they are performing well, to give them positive feedback, to determine what might be impinging on their performance, what training might be deemed necessary and what promotion prospects they might be suitable for.

There are different systems of feedback for different organisations, such as performance-related (usually based on production figures, which would not be suitable in childcare) and judgmental feedback. The expression 'judgmental' should not instil fear in the employee being appraised. Any regular appraisal should be consultative and both employee and supervisor should engage in their own preparation for the process to ensure that discussions are meaningful and productive in terms of staff development, motivation and reward.

Appraisals should:
- Be open and non-threatening.
- Be based on a period of time, not one event.

- Monitor the effectiveness of the setting.
- Provide two-way input.
- Give feedback, not just reprimands.
- Be clear and unambiguous.
- Be equitable and fair.
- Assess training needs.
- Be recorded as a process over time.

When the process is working well, everybody gets a positive result from the appraisal opportunity. It can be accompanied by a self-appraisal process for the childcare worker: they use the same form as you would as supervisor, but they rate themselves on certain criteria agreed as part of the process. They bring this along with them to the appraisal meeting and you compare scores, which can be enlightening for both of you, as you can see where differences in opinion may come from. It can also be very positive for a childcare worker who suffers from poor self-esteem, as your score may be higher than theirs and they will benefit from seeing that others value them more than they do themselves.

It is important that the appraisal process is not confrontational, as this may de-motivate workers. One way of ensuring this is to carry out the process systematically and have it cover a period of time, not just one event. As supervisor, you should also acknowledge positives as well as shortcomings so that the childcare worker does not feel intimidated. One way to do this is to have a ranking system for each category of activity being assessed. For example:

Punctuality

The employee is always on time for work and never leaves before their designated time.

Agree_____ Slightly agree_____ Slightly disagree_____ Disagree_____

Such a format (which takes time to design but is useful in many situations) leaves room for discussion between the appraiser and the appraised. Where possible, a range of questions in this format should be included on the appraisal form as well as a section for suggestions. Such a form could also be useful in exit interviews when staff leave and you want to explore the reasons why.

Motivation

As a supervisor, you will want to know exactly what motivates your staff, as this is where you might need to focus your attention to get fully committed staff. Motivation is about what causes a person to work or behave in a certain way. Putting it in context, it is the desire to do a job rather than the ability to do it (which can be affected by training) or even the resources to do it (which can be supplied by management). There are many theories of motivation and it is beyond the scope of this book to discuss all of them, but we will attempt to explain motivation and its place in the complicated caring profession of childcare.

Abraham Maslow produced a well-known, seminal theory on motivation when he introduced the idea that people to satisfy five different needs.

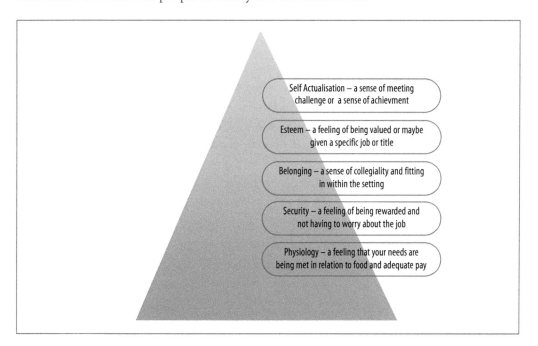

FIGURE 13.1: MASLOW'S HIERARCHY OF NEEDS

This may well determine some motivation issues in your setting, but in the caring professions, some of these are actually less important than the feeling that you are doing something to help others. Childcare is one of those professions where people are often motivated by making the lives of children better, even if the pay is not good.

Frederick Herzberg's two-factor theory of motivation states that there are two classes of factor that motivate people – motivation factors and hygiene factors.

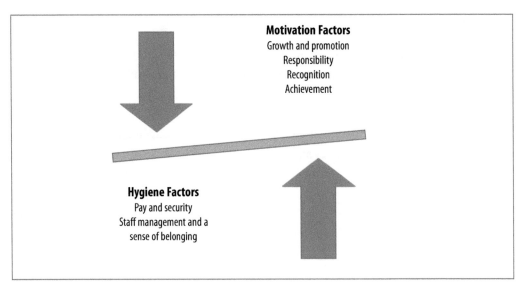

Motivation Factors
Growth and promotion
Responsibility
Recognition
Achievement

Hygiene Factors
Pay and security
Staff management and a
sense of belonging

FIGURE 13.2: HERZBERG'S MOTIVATION AND HYGIENE FACTORS

This theory suggests that focusing on only one aspect of motivation will not produce the results you require, but a combination of hygiene and motivation factors will achieve a balance that will work for the person. This might be more effective in a profession such as childcare, as there are factors such as making children's lives better in the motivation mix.

In his Theory X and Theory Y approach, Douglas McGregor suggested that there are two extremes at which workers operate. Theory X presumes that people do not want to work and only do so if coerced. Theory X also suggests that people do not want to assume responsibility for anything and therefore need to be told what to do. On the other hand, Theory Y is a more positive approach: it suggests that people will be motivated if they feel good about their situation and are receiving rewards; thus you should reward your staff adequately if you want them to perform well. Theory X, on the other hand, suggests that good management will only make people work if everything they do is reviewed and they are told what to do.

The equity theory of motivation is based on the appraisal system. It basically proposes the idea that if our expected inputs are equal to our actual inputs, then our expected outputs should be equal to our expected outputs, and where this happens we will be motivated. This may have more application in an industry where production numbers and wages attached to those numbers are easier to quantify, rather than the childcare profession.

The expectancy theory of motivation assumes that:
● There are a combination of things that motivate people's behaviour.
● Each person has different combinations of needs and desires.

- People control their behaviour by balancing their needs and desires with what they perceive to be a suitable reward for those needs.

In layman's terms, this basically links effort to performance (workers expect they can control this connection), performance to reward, and expectations of fairness to that reward. If everything works together, people will be motivated. This is a complicated concept, with most of the negotiation happening in the worker's head, so it is not easy to put into effect and has limited applicability to the childcare profession.

Actions in childcare are often motivated by the desire to assist children to reach their best potential and to make their lives better. This does not fit easily into a motivation theory that presumes increasing wages will produce better results and is one reason why there are no binding wage agreements in childcare, and very little organisation around wage negotiation. Instead, childcare workers are more concerned with following procedures and regulations.

It is more likely that a combination of many theories will motivate your staff. Only by observing people and their motivators will you as supervisor know how to best motivate your team. This will take some time to establish if you are new to the position or are starting out. Observations of interactions within the team may be the best way to gauge how to motivate the individuals in the team, which could prove to be intrinsic things, such as feelings of belonging, making a difference and helping children live good and productive lives.

Reflective Portfolio Activity

Try to identify what leadership activities take place in your setting, particularly in relation to your own supervisor. Write 500 words on how effective you think this style is in your setting and how you might change it if you were doing the job. Which process of motivation do you think your supervisor is satisfying in adopting their style of leadership?

Leadership Styles

Your ideas about motivation can affect the leadership style you choose. In order to explain this connection, it is necessary to describe the concept of leadership.

Leadership is a process that uses non-pressurised means to motivate behaviour to achieve goals in a team or group setting. It also describes the qualities of a person who has the ability to influence other people's behaviour by being accepted as a leader by the people in the group. The difference between leadership and supervision is that supervision oversees the actions of others, while leadership changes from within the group and often at the same level as those in the group. To see the distinction between the two concepts, look at how change is managed. In supervisory mode, you would look at things that can be done to make sure that benchmarks are met and budgets adhered to, monitor effectiveness of actions and adjust conditions to make sure that the required actions happen. In leadership mode, you would concentrate on working to help people reach their best potential, encouraging and supporting them to do so while equipping them with the skills to make it happen.

There are various theories of leadership that have been put forward after many years of research into the concept.

The trait theory

This assumes that there are specific traits that divide people into leaders and non-leaders. The traits identified by this theory include intelligence, height, self-confidence, vocabulary, achievements and assertiveness. This theory was questioned as it focused on people who were already leaders and tried to interpret what traits they had rather than what traits motivated people to become leaders.

Michigan Leadership Studies

These studies were based on interviews with leaders and followers and developed a two-pronged theory based on the idea that some leaders are job-centred leaders (who concentrate on the job being done by others to improve performance) and others are employee-centred leaders (who concentrate on the combination of people and the job satisfaction of those people). The studies looked at both of these concepts but not at the spectrum in between, which might have created more questions as to where the crossover is between these two concepts.

Situational theories

These theories presume that different situations will generate different leadership behaviours. The behaviours would be a mixture of those analysed in the above theories, but the element of input of any of the above traits or behaviours will depend on the task, the relations in the situation and the element of power the leader has.

No matter what leadership theory is subscribed to, different leadership styles can be seen in most workplaces, and these fall within the concept of situational theories.

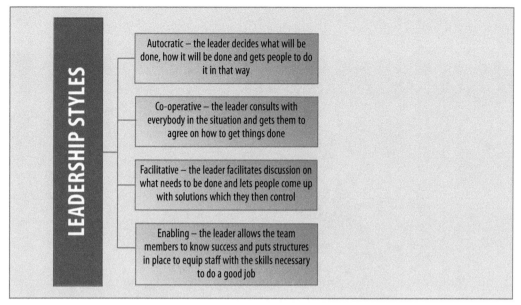

FIGURE 13.3: LEADERSHIP STYLES

Ideas about what motivates people may well influence the type of leadership style adopted. Thus, if you assume that people put money before job satisfaction and belonging, this might lead to an autocratic style of leadership where little is left to interpretation. Your assumptions about motivation may well vary over time and as a leader you may therefore use different styles of leadership in different situations or at different points of team development.

Team Building

A team is a group of people who work as a single unit in a work setting. It may be formed, organic or orchestrated. **Formed teams** are common in work situations, e.g. the staff of the baby room (they have a defined purpose, location and task). **Organic teams** form in a given situation because of the circumstances of the particular situation, e.g. a managerial team where people with different skills get together to make things happen. **Orchestrated teams** form because people have been put in controlled or predictable situations where it is likely that a team will form, e.g. staff sent on a particular type of training that requires specific interactions may well form such a team.

Teams have become a popular form of working and we have already discussed how you might recruit to create a team or replace a person who was a member of a team in order to change the team dynamic.

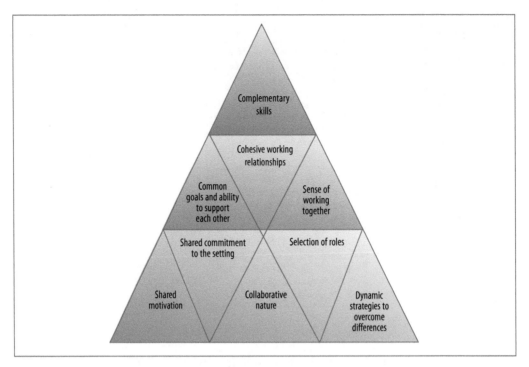

FIGURE 13.4: CONTRIBUTING FACTORS TO TEAM DYNAMICS

However teams are formed, there are clear stages in building teams, which have been identified as follows.

Forming

This is a period of time when people get to know each other. 'Getting to know you' and 'icebreaker' exercises are useful at this stage, as they help to introduce team members to each other.

Storming

The members of the team get to know more about each other and start to test each others' boundaries. There may be conflict around roles and relationships may become fraught as people look for roles for themselves. Leaders may begin to emerge at this stage as people struggle to solve conflicts in the process.

Norming

The team members are finding their own individual roles in the team and defining how they interact with the other members. Compromises are made and roles defined.

Performing

The team gets on with the work. They know who everybody is and what levels of commitment they need to get the job done. They begin to experience success and know the roles everybody is prepared to accept.

There are times when the whole process moves at a different pace, which needs to happen so that the hurdles the team are experiencing are properly addressed: only then can they perform efficiently together. One of the most important teams in any setting is the one that includes the child, their key worker and the parent/guardian. Creating a common goal for such a team is part of the work of every person who works in childcare to ensure that the child reaches their best potential.

While each room in the setting may have its own team, their place is still within the whole team of the setting. Thus, there will be interconnecting associations between teams, which means that the nature of teams is continually changing. Your job as supervisor is to monitor and track such teams to ensure that the child is always at the centre of all work undertaken, but also to provide support and understanding during the storming stage as well as providing challenges at the performing stage.

> **Reflective Portfolio Activity**
> Identify a number of teams in your setting. For each team, write a paragraph about the relationships you see in the team, how they are regulated or controlled and how they work together to meet every child's needs.

Team Roles

Anybody who works with children will be well aware that the childcare team is one where everybody who works with you is part of your team. The interactions of everybody in the team are important, as they give fluidity to the possibilities of what can be done to support children in the setting. By definition, the team works together to get things done, but within this process people often take different roles, which can change depending on the task at hand. Everybody brings different skills to a team, allowing it to move dynamically towards fulfilling its job. The theorist Meredith Belbin categorised team members into the following roles:

- Implementer/leader.
- Shaper (provides drive and focus).
- Completer/finisher.
- Plant (creative innovator).

- Specialist (with the required skills).
- Co-ordinator/facilitator.
- Resource investigator.

Belbin was not the only theorist who looked at team roles, but his have stood the test of time and are still used to understand how and when people take on roles in groups that ensure that it is a group activity rather than an individual enterprise. Each team member will have a number of these skills and will bring them to bear on the work being done by the team. Additionally, the combination of these roles used by each person on the team will depend on the task being done.

To explain this concept further, there may be team members who will take the lead where they feel comfortable with their particular abilities but are happy to take a supportive role in other situations. Fluid roles allow everybody to work comfortably with each other. Sometimes in hierarchical work situations (where there are bosses and subordinates), this process is dictated by the promotion of people in the setting rather than the need for the role in the situation. This can lead to inefficiencies of skills and resources, as time may be wasted in the process of letting somebody lead an activity they may not have the skills to succeed at, while in the meantime the dynamics of interaction in the team are affected by the strain of supporting the process. There may also be overlapping roles, which can cause confusion as to who is actually in the position of leader or motivator, for instance, or even where one person has what they deem to be role overload.

Reflective Portfolio Activity
Look at a routine task that takes place in your setting and identify what team roles are being assumed by individuals involved in the task using Belbin's classification of team roles. Watch the same group perform another activity and observe whether the same people assume similar roles in each activity. If the team roles differ, can you identify what might make the people involved change their roles? Is the changed process more effective in getting the job done? If the roles do not differ, explain why you think they do not and what might be done to support others in changing their roles in the process.

As supervisor, you need to be aware that people will have different levels of team involvement. You need to allow the group to be fluid so that everybody learns, interacts, supports, trusts and believes in the abilities and skill sets within the team and their preferred position in the process. To allow this to happen, you must acknowledge and facilitate changing roles, as such changes will not be evident at the start of the task but will be as it proceeds. The ideal situation you could facilitate is one where everybody gets to have a chance to develop in the process. Perhaps some form of continuous professional development could even be provided that supports people to develop and be comfortable with their roles in any given situation.

Team Working

Getting things done effectively in any setting requires that everybody is prepared to work together in a co-operative way and to share effort, information and skills in a professional manner, for the good of each and every child in the setting. Síolta and Aistear emphasise the need for team working and facilitation in the setting so that the needs of the child are put at the centre of everything being done, which is in keeping with the UNCRC.

Feeling included and valued for your contribution is part of the efficient working of any team and this is especially important in childcare and education, where vulnerability or a sense of insecurity can stifle a person's ability to get the job done. Balancing expectations, behaviour norms, initiative and abilities takes considerable skills on the part of a supervisor, but is necessary to ensure that your team is working well. Added responsibility obviously comes with inter-agency teams, and working in such situations may provide challenges.

As a supervisor, your skills at balancing individual needs, team goals and interpersonal interactions will be required to ensure that every team includes the parents' and children's inputs, as they are partners in the care and education of the child. Internally, you will need to oversee the focus and reporting procedures of each team. Organisationally, you will need to check that the teams are working and interacting well so that internal strife does not stifle efforts or initiatives. Working habits will be set by your organisation, support and design of the individual teams in the setting, and all the work you put into overseeing the flow of information will facilitate a smooth and inclusive system for any team to work within.

Multidisciplinary Teams and Interaction

An example of a multidisciplinary team in a setting could be the involvement of several agencies in supporting a particular child's needs. If one child (or, indeed, several children) deals with an occupational therapist, speech therapist, play therapist and a social worker, each of these people, while involved in a professional capacity, will have their own set of priorities for that child. Balancing these needs in the setting will require considerable professional commitment in ensuring that the priorities of the child come first. Thus, if the occupational therapist has a set of needs in terms of what exercise can be done with the child, it might be possible to incorporate this into the daily routines as long as it can be supported both inside and outside the setting, especially where parents are kept informed.

Ensuring that every discipline is facilitated in the setting is the supervisor's job and interactions must be managed to ensure that time and effort are efficiently spent with the child. For example, if a child needs to practise speech on a daily basis as recommended by their speech therapist, the child's routine could be changed, with your support and the key worker's efforts, to include this practice.

Some professionals who may interact with a child include:

- Psychologist
- Public health nurse
- Physiotherapist
- Speech therapist
- Occupational therapist
- Language specialist
- Interpreter

One of the advantages of having facilities for such multidisciplinary teams in a setting is that the child does not have to leave the setting for appointments and miss other things that happen in the setting. In addition, parents don't have to leave work to bring the child to different locations for appointments because you as supervisor have set in place the systems that allow such activities to happen in the setting. The child is used to having routines that make them feel safe and secure and this incorporates all their needs in a familiar setting and is geared to them having their preferences and individual rights acknowledged, as envisaged by Síolta.

FOURTEEN

Communication

Communication is a process of transferring information and is an important part of Síolta and Aistear in the ECCE setting. The principle of open communication is embraced in the Síolta principles of teamwork, the role of the adult, working with parents and the rights of the child. Standard 12 of Síolta sets out the signposts you need to examine in relation to communication in the setting. Additionally, the need to communicate, and specifically to teach children to communicate, is one of the themes of Aistear.

Communication is multifaceted and there are several dimensions that need to be addressed in a quality setting. Anybody who is familiar with the Diageo TV advert for Arthur's Day will see the difference between a message that is given and one that is received: in the advert a toast is raised 'to Arthur' and this is interpreted a little further down the road as 'to Martha'. This illustrates the concept of effective communication – making sure that the message that is received is the message that was sent. There are many factors that influence both the sender and the receiver in the process of communication.

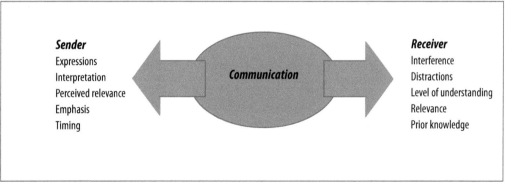

FIGURE 14.1: COMMUNICATION

The most sophisticated forms of communication will fail if the receiver is not willing to listen. This is especially important in verbal communication, as the whole message may be ignored if understanding of the message is not complete. Ensuring that the people who are receiving the communication are paying attention, asking questions to check that they understand, have no prejudices and can understand why the message is being said adds to the effectiveness of the communication that is taking place.

Interpersonal Communication

Interpersonal communication takes place between people. There are different forms of communication: oral, written and non-verbal.

Oral communication is used most often in daily life. It is quick, you know that the person has received the message and it facilitates an easy response. The popularity of Skype shows how important we find face-to-face communication as a means of keeping in touch with people. Oral communication is an effective means of getting messages across, provided that the sender does not use the wrong words, tone, timing or place – background noise, for example, can interfere with the message – and it also does not always allow you time to consider your answer and perhaps be diplomatic where necessary.

Written communication methods include cards, letters, reports, memos, emails and texts. Written communication is less immediate because there is a time gap between when the message is written and when it is read.

Non-verbal communication includes music, pictures, videos, posters and body language (hugs, sighs, shrugs, etc.). Such forms of communication can have the disadvantage of being open to misinterpretation.

Picking the right form of communication is important for both the receiver and the sender and the choice of method is often influenced by the situation in which the communication takes place. Many people have email on the move nowadays, but that can mean that if you send an email at an inconvenient time there may be a delay before you get an answer.

Different forms of communication are appropriate in different situations. For example, the minutes of a meeting should be written, but passing on your condolences to a friend after a bereavement should be done orally.

The method of communication must be carefully considered to ensure that the message is properly understood and, more important, that it is welcome, interpreted correctly and capable of getting the job done.

Communication in the ECCE setting is important, as you are communicating with children, parents, staff and outside agencies, each with different characteristics and requirements. For this reason, any interpersonal communication should consider the personal circumstances, needs and understanding capabilities of each person being communicated with. Only then should the method be chosen, as it is not 'one size fits all', and several methods may do the job better than just one, e.g. a cartoon for children and a written notice for parents. At all stages, you as supervisor must also consider the content of the message being relayed, as this may dictate the format best suited for the delivery of the message.

> ### Reflective Portfolio Activity
> Parents often visit settings, with or without their child, before deciding on the one most suitable for the child. During these visits, parents often receive a handbook that tells them what they might expect if their child enrols. What do you think should be given to a visiting child on such occasions so that they know what to expect? What format would you use to give information to children with different understanding, reading and writing abilities about what will happen in their day and the activities that take place so that they feel secure? Design and create something that you could give children in this situation and explain why you chose this method.

Flows of information, which, as we have seen, will include much group communication, are also important in the setting. Examples of communication flows include the following.

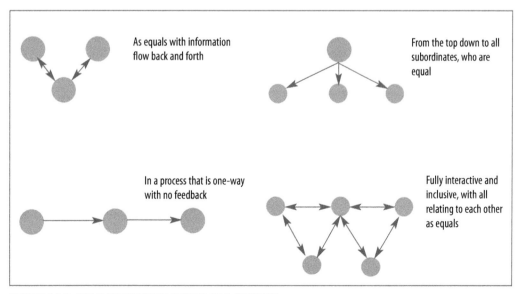

FIGURE 14.2: COMMUNICATION FLOWS IN A SETTING

The type of communication flow depend on the numbers involved and the working style of the setting. The flow may vary according to the dynamics of the team or indeed the task being undertaken and it will depend on the team roles everybody has assumed for the task in hand. Leadership style may also affect the type of communication flow that is predominant in the setting: an autocratic leader may favour one method, and a democratic leader another. As supervisor, you need to be fully aware of the possibilities each occasion to communicate offers you in terms of the message, the way it is transmitted and ultimately how it is received.

Consulting Stakeholders

Looking at the different methods of communication flow, it is easy to see that the method will depend on who is being communicated with. One of the most important flows of information in a setting is the flow from stakeholders to the setting and vice versa. The characteristics of the stakeholder may determine the method of communication used.

As supervisor, you must familiarise yourself with the preferred method of communication for each stakeholder, as this is the best way to ensure that your message and their responses are properly understood. Additionally, each stakeholder may have different needs that require you to vary your communication style. An example would be parents who speak different languages and need things interpreted or who have specific needs based on disability or an inability to read or write. You must be aware of the possibilities, which may sometimes mean that information will be conveyed in more than one way on any given day. Another example is where menus for the week are graphically displayed and also sent home in a written format.

The example we gave earlier of the parents and the child visiting the setting to decide whether to enrol the child was an example of how information can be prepared for stakeholders that meets their needs. Similarly, in a community location posters can be used to let people know what to expect in the setting. The possibilities are endless as long as you are open to discussion and thought.

Getting feedback should be a regular activity in any setting and it should be meaningful and productive if you want to be sure that the quality assurance you have put in place is doing the required job. Comment boxes do not always work unless they are positioned sensitively. People often feel too intimidated to put comments in comment boxes for fear that they can be identified by their handwriting. If you have put systems in place to work with stakeholders – such as committees, consultation groups, forums or other interactive systems – you will be able to judge what form of communication best suits each group. It is a constant process and helps people to feel that their opinions are valued. More important, they will also feel free to let you know if you are inadvertently missing some fundamental problem that may be developing and this may indeed be a way of resolving potential conflicts.

Reflective Portfolio Activity

Look at the ways in which information is communicated in your setting under the following headings:

▶ Children

▶ Parents

▶ Staff

▶ Community

▶ Visitors

Explain the different communication methods used under each heading and discuss how effective you feel each method used is. Discuss which don't work and explain what you would do differently if you were a supervisor in the setting. Summarise your piece by discussing the benefits of effective communication methods in a childcare and early education setting.

Delegation

As you will have realised in reading this book, the job of a supervisor is one that carries with it many responsibilities and a need to keep informed about everything that is going on in the setting and how it impacts on the children and others. Methods, systems, time management and other skills are needed so that things happen when and how they are planned to happen. The job is so encompassing that there is a distinct need to allow others to do some parts of it and report to you, for example in a key worker system where one person works closely with the child but keeps you informed of changes and developments with that child. This involves a system of delegation.

Delegation is a process of allowing others to take responsibility for parts of a process for which you retain overall responsibility. Some people find it difficult to delegate because they feel they are letting go of some of their responsibilities and they do not trust others to do as good a job as them. In some situations this may well be the case, but it can be rectified with good groundwork.

Some of the reasons why people avoid delegating to others include:

● Loss of control.

● Having ultimate responsibility if things go wrong.

● Doubt in the other person's abilities.

- Inability to influence all decisions.
- Lack of procedures for feedback.
- Poor organisational systems.

Reasons why delegation does work include:
- Getting a very detailed job done in small parts which can be added together.
- Stress relief.
- Building management capabilities in your team.
- Freeing time to work on other issues.
- Building effective teams.
- It makes people feel a valued part of the setting and valued.

Unless you as supervisor want to be in 20 places at once, you will need to develop some ability and confidence in the process of delegation. If it is properly done, you will still be in a position to take overall responsibility for things that happen in the setting, as delegation should never be a process of allowing others to take blame when it rightly belongs with you.

Ways to ensure that you develop your delegation procedures include:
- Knowing your staff well and observing their strengths and weaknesses so that you know what they can do well and what they might avoid if they can.
- Defining the work in easy-to-understand terms and procedures.
- Giving clear and unambiguous descriptions of the nature and scope of the work being delegated, with clear guidelines on what is and is not included.
- Ensuring that the person you delegate to has the tools and support to do the job.
- Accepting that sometimes the person to whom you delegate may be able to do a better job than you.
- Facilitating co-operation in the team to support a person who is accepting new responsibilities and having an open door policy should problems occur.
- Setting up regular reporting opportunities and showing initiative where you suspect help would be appreciated.
- Praising the positives and supporting the negatives in the process and remembering that there is a learning curve for everybody.
- Being patient and supportive throughout.

You will be surprised at how, with planning, support and feedback, your team will be able to support each other in getting everything done and how you will be able to put procedures in place that facilitate good working relationships in the setting.

Meetings

As we have just discussed delegation, with the assumption that meetings will take place to pass over responsibilities and to give feedback, it is timely to introduce the concept of meetings. Meetings will take place in settings for any number of reasons and they may be formal (such as those with other professionals) or informal (a conversation or reporting opportunity with colleagues). Whatever the format, every meeting should be recorded and the information shared.

Formal meetings should include the following.

Agreement on timing

Make sure the people who need to be at the meeting can fit it into their timetable. This means that some arrangements may have to be made to facilitate the people who need to be there to make sure they're free.

Prior agenda distribution

Everybody should know what is going to be discussed at the meeting so that they have a chance to prepare. This also means that time is not wasted at the meeting giving background information when this could be included in the agenda. An agenda simply records the time and place of the meeting as well as what format the discussions will take. Time limits can also be set for some topics to ensure that there is time to discuss everything on the agenda.

The following is an example of an agenda.

Meeting of Parents' Committee of Everyday Childcare Centre
Committee Room, Wednesday, 21 November, 7.30 p.m.

Agenda
1. Minutes of previous meeting to be read and approved
2. New staff appointments
3. Fundraising requirements (report attached)
4. Parents' feedback
5. Any other business (AOB)

As you can see, the points are brief and succinct. Any background information can be included with the agenda so that business can move quickly at the meeting.

Reading the previous meeting's record and agreement

As the minutes of any meeting are usually done directly after the meeting has taken place, everybody should check that the details recorded are an accurate account of what actually happened. In order to ensure this, everybody should vote to accept the minutes and sign them as being accurate so that everything is transparent.

Recording processes and attendance

This is a brief summary of discussions that take place at the meeting and should be accurate in its interpretation of each person's contributions to the discussions. The recording process is to ensure that if extra things are added to the decision-making process there is a record of where those ideas or suggestions came from.

Agreement on delegation of activities

Inevitably, decisions will be made and people who have the necessary skills to help get the job done will volunteer to assist in the process. There should be agreement that those people are involved and to what extent. If they need help to get the job done, this should also be recorded.

Jonathan agreed to speak to the parents on an individual basis to get suggestions and will report back to the next meeting.

Jennifer volunteered to seek the views of a representative group of children to judge their needs going forward.

Etc.

Summary of agreed tasks

Meetings often cover a range of issues that may or may not have agreed actions by the end of the meeting and all such tasks should be noted so that they can be checked back on later. Where no action was agreed, this should also be noted, as the discussion could have been put back to another meeting.

TABLE 14.1

Item	Agreed	By Whom	By When
1	Check with parents	Jonathan	29 November
2	Ask children	Jennifer Supported by:	29 November

This gives a timeframe for any decisions, which gives momentum to processes to make the agreed actions happen.

Conclusion

Meetings should have conclusions so that discussions do not become a drawn-out process. It is the chairperson's job to make sure that there is a chance for new business to be introduced, which is done under Any Other Business (AOB). After that, a summary of actions agreed should be read and the meeting drawn to a conclusion with an agreed indicative date for the next meeting.

The minutes

Minutes will be recorded during the meeting but formalised afterwards for approval at the next meeting.

At the end of every meeting, there should be a feeling of having achieved something and that there is a sense of purpose bring agreed actions to completion. This makes for efficient meetings, which, more important, get things happening. An effective meeting creates an inclusive environment and ensures that consultation takes place and views are sought, which allows children's rights and preferences to be part of any activities in the setting, as required by the principles and standards of Síolta.

The reporting requirements of the Child Care (Pre-School Services) (No. 2) (Amendment) Regulations 2006, together with Síolta and Aistear and your own quality assurance processes, all contribute to the need to keep accurate records of actions, reasons for and consequences of everything that is agreed in the setting. For these reasons, records should be kept safe and secure for as long as possible. If kept on computer, they should be encrypted to protect the details of those involved in the process.

Reflective Portfolio Activity

As a team, set up a meeting to design and create a newsletter for distribution to parents and children for the autumn term. In the meeting:

▶ Agree on contents, methods and distribution.

▶ Agree on a design and how it will be produced.

▶ Include children, parents and staff in the process.

▶ Inform parents and children of what will happen and when during the term.

▶ Make the newsletter interesting.

▶ Assign activities to everybody in the group.

▶ Keep minutes and list any other meetings that should take place in the process.

▶ Use agendas, task lists, due dates and minutes to record the process.

Meetings should be held regularly and when the process is clearly understood they will become part of the routine of every supervisor.

Conflict Resolution

Where interactions take place in any setting and people need to either work with others or compromise to get things done, there is potential for conflict. Conflict is about disagreement and can be either productive or destructive.

TABLE 14.2: PRODUCTIVE AND DESTRUCTIVE ELEMENTS OF CONFLICT

Productive Elements of Conflict	Destructive Elements of Conflict
• It can act as an impetus for more activity.	• It can stifle activity and creativity.
• It can focus people on the task at hand.	• It can create a hostile environment.
• It can make people want to succeed.	• It can cause stress.
• It can be a motivator.	• It can interfere with proven processes.
• It can get the job done more efficiently.	• It can de-motivate.

It is important for any supervisor to be aware of conflict and to measure its effects on productivity in the setting. Watching interactions between groups and individuals may indicate that there is a mismatch between the people involved, but also there can be conflict between individuals and the setting's goals that need to be resolved.

Some of the factors that contribute to conflict may include:

● Feelings of not being valued.

● Having a high opinion of one's abilities.

- Differences of conscience.
- Failure to include a person in the decision-making process.
- Stress of too much responsibility being borne by one person.
- Lack of information needed to do a good job.
- Distrust of motives.
- Jealousy.
- Feeling of being taken for granted.

This list is not exhaustive, but it gives an idea of the breadth of possible causes that need to be monitored in any setting. People deal with conflict in different ways. Some embrace the possibility to compromise, while others may refuse to compromise, blame others, withdraw, resent, gang up or use other isolation strategies.

As supervisor, you need to take control of anything that is affecting the working of your setting, and this includes conflict. The method of conflict resolution you use may be based on the assumptions or observations you make about the possible causes of the conflict. There are a number of strategies you can consider, as each cause of conflict may require different strategies:

- Break the conflict into its constituent parts and address each piece of the problem.
- Never look just for fault, as there are usually other issues at play.
- Change the situations that are contributing to the escalation of conflict.
- Address each party separately to get explanations for what is happening.
- Involve the people experiencing the conflict to suggest solutions that you could consider.
- Renegotiate the terms that are causing the problem.
- Redesign the teams so that people adopt different roles in the group and thus avoid whatever was causing the conflict.
- Be sensitive to issues that may be personal and have nothing to do with the setting, and offer support to ease stress.
- Have a mentoring process in place that is designed to negotiate on such issues of conflict that arise, as this helps balance the needs of the setting and those of the individuals involved.
- If all else fails, bring in an outside mediator who has skills in conflict resolution.

There will often be a time of trial and error in conflict resolution, but it is worth the effort involved if you can achieve a fully functioning setting where everybody feels valued, appreciated and can contribute to the best of their ability.

Reflective Portfolio Activity

Look at some issues that have contributed to a feeling of conflict for you in the setting you are working in. Examine what has been done about the conflict you experienced and how effective it was in eliminating the problem. What would you do differently if you were the supervisor? Explain how this would have eliminated the problem in a different way.

Bullying

There are often conflicts in a workplace that do not have an easy resolution and continue to cause problems over a period of time, and bullying can fit into this category. There are significant effects on individuals who are bullied and these can impact on their ability to work and learn in any setting where the problems are left unresolved. Bullying is engaging in a behaviour that is likely to cause another person to feel uncomfortable or hurt. For the most part it is a deliberate act that has a pattern and is not usually a one-off situation.

Bullying happens everywhere in society, so it is no surprise that you as supervisor may be called upon to mediate in bullying cases between children and also between adults. The new *Children First* guidelines have a specific section on bullying, which they define as 'repeated aggression – whether it is verbal, psychological or physical – that is conducted by an individual or group against others. It is behaviour that is intentionally aggravating and intimidating, and occurs mainly among children in social environments such as schools'. This is not a phenomenon that is limited to children – adults can be both victims and perpetrators of bullying too.

The effects of bullying include:

- Inability to function in the environment.
- Low self-esteem.
- Being held back in progress.
- Inability to contribute to the setting.
- Physical injuries in some cases.
- Psychological damage.
- Inability to meet challenges because of fear it may escalate the bullying.
- Being left out and isolated.
- Feelings of not being in control of your life.

The effects are significant and every childcare and early education setting is required to have stated policies and procedures to deal with bullying under the Child Care (Pre-

School Services) (No. 2) (Amendment) Regulations 2006. The processes set out in the procedures must be understood by all stakeholders and should be clearly displayed in the setting. Every setting should check that all stakeholders understand the policy and should be engaged enough to have the tools and procedures to report it, and indeed to expect that something will be done about it. As supervisor, you should use strategies such as those outlined in the section on conflict resolution above to address inter-staff bullying when it is brought to your attention – if you have not already been observant enough to spot it.

Whether it is children or adults who are bullying in your setting, you need to use some strategies that encourage those who feel they are being bullied to seek assistance in the setting:

- Listening properly and acknowledging the person's feelings.
- Encouraging discussions around the topic to show that there is an awareness that it could happen.
- Empowering people in their daily interactions in the setting.
- Being patient.
- Considering the possibilities.
- Acknowledging the victim's rights.
- Addressing the problem.
- Showing respect.
- Sorting the problem.
- Putting strategies in place so that it does not happen again.

FIFTEEN

Transitions

A period of transition is a time of change. As children are so dependent on others in any setting, the process of transition can be a worrying one for everybody. They are required to move from what they know and have mastered to another situation in which they need to learn their place all over again. Adults also go through transitions, such as starting a new job, and feel uncomfortable in doing so. All the apprehension an adult feels is multiplied several times for a child, as they cannot usually express their feelings or even understand what the feeling is.

During a period of transition, everything in your environment changes and the support structures you had in place are no longer of any use. You have to set up new support structures, introduce yourself to new concepts and learn new rules of engagement. The younger the child, the more unhappy this fear of the unknown will make them to feel. Standards 13 and 14 of Síolta require that we take into account the child's fears around transitions and their sense of identity and belonging. This also fits in with Aistear's theme of identity and belonging in a curriculum framework. Both Síolta and Aistear also require that we keep and transfer information with the child to support continuity of care and education as the child moves from one phase to another.

Types of Transition

Children experience many different types of transition, which can have an impact on their understanding of normality and can throw their world into disarray. Such transitions include the following.

Change from pre-school to school

A child may not know what to expect in the new school and may need to get to know a whole new group of friends, as the other children in the setting may not be moving to the same school.

A new house

A child may be apprehensive about the size of the house, whether Santa can find them, whether they will be able to keep their friends, whether other people in the area will be friendly or whether they might have to get a bus to and from the setting. They might also worry about the new neighbourhood and even the distance from their grandparents or extended family.

Parents separating

Children may worry that they were at fault. They might also be worried about being able to visit each parent or that the other parent will be lonely without them.

A new family group

Mum or Dad could be settling with a new partner and the child may not know who will look after them. They may worry about whether or not the new person in their lives will love them, and if the new partner has children of their own there may be a worry about being one of a group.

A new sibling

Will the new child change their relationship with the parents? Will the new child take their toys and eat their food? Will the new child like them? Will they like the new child?

Death

Will the person never be able to come back to see them? What happens to the body? Could they have done something to stop the person dying? Will they be allowed to be happy or will they ever be happy? Can they still tell jokes? Will the person who has died be looking at them all the time from somewhere?

Change of key worker

Who will they talk to? Who will make sure they reach their goals? Who will replace them? Will they like the new person? If not, what will they be able to do about it?

Moving from one group to another in the setting

Moving from a wobbler room to a toddler room can be upsetting for a child, as they may not be able to do the same activities they did in the wobbler room and now they are expected to master other skills without some of their friends who may not be making the move just yet.

While some of the worries can be easily answered, the child must feel they can ask questions and get real answers. They may spend considerable time asking new versions of the same question as they are trying to find out if you really mean the answer you gave them, which means they don't have to worry. Remember that the child may not have the words to ask the questions, as in the case of very young children, but they will still go through a stage of transition that can upset them.

Preparation

Finding out about the transition is the greatest asset in preparing a child for any new situation in their life. Regularly talking to parents and the child and listening for new developments in their lives will alert you to possible transitions that are about to happen in the child's life.

Preparation is the greatest antidote to the fear of transition in any setting and there are many strategies that can be put in place to improve the change process for a child. It is important to ease the child's fears, as they will then be better able to move on in the setting or life situation and will adapt more quickly to the new circumstances. This is especially important in the school change situation, as the child can get on with learning, rather than worrying needlessly, and they can make friends more quickly in the new setting, which helps them feel secure again.

Putting yourself in the child's situation will allow you to anticipate some of the worries the child may have and you can then help them, even if the child is unable to voice the exact emotions they are feeling.

Enabling Moving Forward

The preparations you put in place that will allow a child to move confidently into the new situation can include the following.

Change from pre-school to school

Visit the new setting with the key worker and get to know the layout and where you will be every day; learn to sit still while doing activities (gradually build this up so that the child will be able to behave in the classroom); learn to put your hand up to ask a question; know where the toilet is and who to ask to go; get introduced to other children who have made a similar move from the setting to the school and see that they are happy; ask questions and feel secure that the questions will be answered.

A new house

Maybe get Mum or Dad to explain what is good about the house; have a picture of what it looks like so that the child can discuss it in the setting and show it to other children; assure the child that they can still get to the setting if that is still possible; look at maps of the area in their curriculum work; and see what is in the area that the child will like.

Parents separating

Remind a child that their parents still love them even if they cannot live together; discuss the excitement of visiting each parent and having them invite them to stay; discuss if they can bring toys and what will be in each parent's house so that they are aware that they will still have familiar things and routines.

A new family

Remind the child that they have friends in the setting and that it is a type of family; discuss what new children will be there and talk about ways to get to know new people; ensure the child is able to express their feelings and knows how to ask for help if it is needed; talk to and support parents, who will also have worries and may be worried for the child.

A new sibling

Show and discuss different family groups; point out the positives of having a sibling; explain that it will not make any difference to how you will treat the child; assure the child that their parents will still love them and will play with them again as soon as they also get used to the new child.

Death

This is one that should be sensitively approached with the parents' approval. You could explain that it is a natural part of life. Explain what will happen and that it is all right to feel sad, but that it is also all right to feel happy afterwards, as the person who dies would want them to be happy and would be happy that they are.

Change of key worker

Assure the child that they can still see the key worker (if that is the case) and that the new key worker will have taken lots of notes on their preferences from the other key worker. Acknowledge their fears and assure them that the process of them being at the centre of everything being done will not change, and that they will soon feel happy and secure again.

Moving from one stage to another in the setting

The child will be reassured if they are welcome to come back to visit, can go on trips to the new room for short periods and can bring along something that makes them feel secure until they are used to the new surroundings. They can visit their friends and can still play with them outside on the swing or slide.

In all cases, the preparation and thought that goes into the process reassures the child and enables them to make the transition quickly and efficiently and settle into their new situation with the assurance that people still care for them in the same way.

Supporting the Child's Development

Being confident in new surroundings means that the child can reach their potential and also feel secure that problems can be solved and that their worries are taken seriously. They will quickly embrace change and be in a position to continue with their development milestones. Fear can disable a child, and for a child who has additional needs, a transition may be more traumatic, as they will have extra worries about whether those needs will be met and who will assist them. Change should be part of a child's life, as new experiences allow them to learn new skills in new settings. Being confident, or at the very least feeling less worried, means that the child can embrace change in the future and see that there are ways of solving problems if you look at the worries first and help develop strategies to overcome them.

A child may be encouraged to bring a transition item to the new setting, but this may not always be necessary and the time spent visiting the new setting may be enough to dispel most fears. Knowing how to voice fears as part of a transition is important in a child's development and your preparation work will produce results that last a lifetime.

SIXTEEN

Legislation

Health and Safety

Health and safety legislation applies to every aspect of the setting, as we saw in Chapter 4 on setting up and planning your own setting. Every child's rights are protected if the setting adheres to the requirements set out under legislation and there are serious penalties where breaches of the law occur. Under Síolta, the requirement to look after the health and safety of every child in the setting comes under Standards 1, 2, 9 and 15, and this requirement supports the well-being theme in Aistear.

Every setting must adhere to procedures that they have a part in writing to make sure that things done in the setting satisfy any legal requirements. This also applies to ensuring that the regulations regarding numbers and space are applied, as this will reduce the risk of accidents and limit potential stress: children need space and a high level of interaction with their environment.

Space is not the only consideration in the setting – procedures for many activities come under the heading of health and safety. Under the Safety, Health and Welfare Act 2005, there are specific rules for the workplace that should be familiar to any supervisor in any setting. These considerations should be further informed by the Safety, Health and Welfare at Work (General Application) Regulations 2007, which set out standards for many features in the workplace. Every setting must carry out a risk assessment procedure and develop procedures to be followed to minimise the potential harm that may be caused by any risk identified. Everybody should be involved in the process of risk assessment and every setting should have a risk assessment statement that details the risk and the procedures agreed by the work setting. All workers must sign this and the procedures laid out must be followed rigorously.

The requirements for health and safety in any pre-school setting will be examined as part of any HSE inspection that takes place, and because of the vulnerability of children, this is appropriate: nothing should be left to chance. However, there are requirements in relation to staff, such as non-intoxicant policies and no smoking policies, and every setting must put the health and safety of all stakeholders at the forefront of their activities. A copy of the Safety, Health and Welfare Act 2005 should be available in the setting and should be regularly reviewed, with any changes in policy or procedures highlighted and quickly implemented.

Fire Safety

A Fire Officer will inspect the plans for the setting and visit before start-up to oversee any issues that may arise. Every setting must have fire safety equipment in each room and ensure that regular fire drills are held and recorded. As a rule of thumb, a fire drill should happen:

- When a new child starts.
- When a new member of staff joins.
- When students are taken on for work placements.
- At least every month in other situations.
- Sooner if there was a problem with the last drill.

To put it simply, every man, woman, child and visitor in the setting should know what to do in a fire drill. Every escape route must be kept clear and should not be locked or inaccessible, and the register of owners and contactable people should be up to date and available for inspection.

Equipment in each room must be regularly maintained and records must be kept of when fire drills took place, any issues that arose and how it is proposed to deal with those issues. Under the Fire Services Act 1981 and Fire Safety in Pre-schools Guidelines 1999, the Fire Officer will check that fire alarms and smoke detectors, fire blankets, extinguishers and other safety devices are adequate for your requirements and suitably placed and that your internal announcement systems are adequate to deal with any issues that may arise, as we have already pointed out in this book. Remember that failure to satisfy a Fire Officer that there is a robust attitude to fire safety can result in your setting being closed down, either for good or until any required work is completed.

Hygiene

Any workplace has hygiene requirements, but the vulnerability of babies and children to infection makes hygiene in the workplace even more important in a pre-school setting. Policies and procedures must include the following.

- Cleaning rosters and responsibilities are clearly signposted.
- Staff maintain high levels of personal hygiene.
- Infectious disease policies are adhered to.

- Toys are regularly cleaned.
- Children appreciate the need to be hygienic in the setting and know how to wash their hands regularly, cover their mouths when they cough and understand that sometimes it is best for them to stay at home if they feel unwell.
- Procedures and routines in relation to beds and sleeping areas are followed.
- Appropriate temperatures are maintained to minimise the risk of infection.
- Surfaces are promptly cleaned after spills.
- Fridges are kept at adequate temperatures.
- Food preparation areas are out of the reach of children.
- Foods are properly cooked and any area where food is prepared is of adequate standard to reduce the risk of infection.

As you can see, there are many hygiene factors in any setting and all staff should be well versed, as part of their induction and training, in the need for good hygiene standards in the setting. Regular inspections will be carried out by the Environmental Health Officer to check compliance in this important area. Failure to satisfy the inspector that there is a good system to ensure hygiene in the setting can result in a closure order on a temporary or permanent basis in the interests of children's and public health. Records of inspections and outcomes must be available for inspection on the premises under Regulation 5 of the Child Care (Pre-School Services) (No. 2) (Amendment) Regulations 2006, together with copies of all relevant Acts in relation to the operation of a pre-school setting.

Empowering Children

Children in the setting have a part to play in ensuring that they understand their rights under Síolta (Standards 1, 12, 15) and under the Aistear theme of communicating. A child should be able to let people know when something is bothering them and they should know how to express their feelings in such a way as to be easily understood.

Speaking to children about their abilities and rights, building their self-esteem and taking on board their individual preferences all support and empower children to protect themselves in any setting where they may feel uncomfortable. As supervisor, this is an important responsibility and requires you to ensure that you and everybody in the setting listens carefully to children in order to empower them to state their wishes and expect them to be observed.

Letting children know about potential dangers in a way that doesn't frighten them is a delicate and specialised skill that your staff should have, and supporting questions children may have in relation to risks means that that each child can make informed decisions in relation to their own safety and protection. Remember that under the

UNCRC, every child has the right to be heard and to express their views at a level that is consistent with their age and stage of development. Somebody can only judge this if they know the child's potential, and the supervisor along with the key worker are well placed to make sure this happens.

These precautions now extend to online activities and small children's access to the internet via their mobile phones. Children should be carefully instructed on the dangers of giving out too much information about themselves and on respecting others who do not want to share information. Supervision is required in this area and you should be supportive of parents who may be too relaxed in areas that might pose significant risks for children.

SEVENTEEN

Community and the ECCE Setting

E very ECCE setting operates in an area that has distinct characteristics that may or may not have shaped the nature of the service. It may be a community setting that has been shaped by the people and the area or it may have started as a profit-making setting and have been influenced by the people from the area who have availed of the service.

Belonging to a Community

Children thrive on the concept of understanding, and being part of their surroundings and their community is a big part of who they are and indeed who they might become. When we teach children about their rights, this is firmly based on a sense of belonging to a wider community of individuals in society. We have already stated that the community around the setting is a stakeholder in the setting, as they have mutual impacts on each other and each other's operations. Shops, doctors, dentists, libraries, theatres and other services exist in the community and children engage with these when they are not in the setting. Children talk about their interactions with the community and being able to feel comfortable in their relationships requires all stakeholders to be consulted, as we discussed earlier.

Aistear's theme on identity and belonging requires us to engage with the child's community as part of their early learning curriculum. Under Regulation 5, records are required to be kept on children's interests and these should be incorporated into later work with the child on the curriculum.

Other agencies in children's lives

Some children have complicated lives and sometimes, as we discussed in the section on multi-agency working, there are other agencies involved in children's lives outside the setting. Some of these may engage directly with the setting, such as those already discussed, but others may have an independent relationship with the child, such as:

- **Barnardos:** A support and advocacy agency for children's rights and needs.
- **Childline:** For children who may need support to deal with something that is worrying them and who cannot or have not discussed it with anybody else.
- **AA services:** For parents who have alcohol dependencies.
- **Focus Ireland:** Who may be assisting the family to get a home.
- **Enable Ireland:** Provide services for children with disabilities.
- **Doctors and hospitals:** Children may have appointments they need to keep in relation to short- or long-term health problems.
- **Local businesses:** Children's families may be involved in the area and may be creating employment for others.
- **Community services:** Museums, libraries, exhibitions, etc.

The possible interactions in the community are endless and it should therefore be part of the supervisor's work to engage with some of these agencies in the best interest of the children involved. Getting to know what is going on and how it can be supported will help the child's future interactions. Knowing that the setting supports their needs is important and enabling for all children.

Co-operation

Agencies that engage with children from the setting are also charged with protecting their safety and welfare. Offering support in such situations is not the same as breaching a child's privacy; it is about enabling the best intervention to happen within your capabilities and the resources of the other agency or agencies.

Your setting may have meeting rooms available for interventions that support the child or the family. Everybody will benefit, as the child will be secure and feel that their wishes and needs are being supported, but it is vital that confidences are kept with the relevant agency, as this ensures their professional approach. Care should be taken, but the intervention in a child's life may create better opportunities for that child going forward.

When requested, every professional courtesy should be extended and the best interests of the child should be the primary concern of everybody involved.

Facilitation

Allowing services that engage with children to support the child in the setting environment will save time for the child and the parents. However, community involvement in the setting does not just relate to outside agencies using your services. It could also involve the community agency providing support to the children in the setting as part of a curriculum activity.

An example of this would be inviting a fire brigade crew to visit the setting or arranging a visit to their establishment. This might happen around Hallowe'en, when children can be informed about the need to be safe around bonfires (being careful that the delivery is not too graphic for the age group). A local theatre group could devise a performance that would support the visit and the children can both learn about the level of responsibility they have in relation to the own well-being and gain a sense of independence and identity. This can be recorded as part of a curriculum activity under Aistear and Regulation 5 of the Child Care (Pre-School Services) (No. 2) (Amendment) Regulations 2006.

Extended Experiences

Challenging children in the setting is part of the early education concept. Children will go through different stages during the time they are in the setting and as supervisor you must be willing to extend the experience within the community for the sake of the individual child's abilities.

When a child learns to count, they also learn about money as part of a play activity that matches Aistear's theme of identity and belonging. Once children have grasped the concept of money, you may be able to extend that experience by bringing them on a walk to get a feel for spending money in a real setting and your local shopkeeper may help. Children in the setting will see how the setting empowers them and allows them to scaffold and reinforce their learning. The community-based shop may get extra business as parents visit too.

Correctly planned and incorporated into the curriculum, these opportunities to bring learning outside the setting will ensure that children and others engage with a range of activities. The parents may gradually be included in the process and then the child will see that all elements of their community are involved in their learning.

References

Belbin, B.M., *Management Teams: Why They Succeed or Fail*, Oxford: Butterworth-Heinemann, 1981.

Department of Children and Youth Affairs, *Children First: National Guidance for the Protection and Welfare of Children*, Dublin: Department of Children and Youth Affairs, 2011.

Department of Education and Science, *Siolta, the National Quality Framework for Early Childhood Education*, Dublin: Department of Education and Science, 2010.

Hertzberg, F., *The Motivation to Work*, New York: John Wiley & Sons, 1959.

Maslow, A., 'A Theory of Human Motivation', *Psychology Review*, Vol. 50, 1943, 370–96.

McGregor, D., *Proceedings of the Fifth Anniversary Convocation of Industrial Management, The Human Side of Enterprise*, Boston, MA: Massachusetts Institute of Technology, 1957.

National Council for Curriculum and Assessment, *Aistear: The Early Childhood Curriculum Framework*, Dublin: National Council for Curriculum and Assessment, 2009.

Index